BOOK ONE

THE MASTERS OF HORSEMANSHIP
S E R I E S

A GUIDEBOOK FOR
THE ROAD
TO SUCCESS

◆

Alfred Knopfhart

The Masters of Horsemanship Series, Book One

Dressage: *A Guidebook for the Road to Success* by Alfred Knopfhart

© 1996 Half Halt Press, Inc.

Published as **Dressur von A-S, *4. Auflage*** © by Muller Ruschlikon Verlags AG, Gewerbestrasse 10, CH-6330 Cham.

Illustrations by Marianne Merz

The editors wish to thank Michelle Clayton and Ulrike Taylor for their invaluable assistance with translation.

Printed in the United States of America

ISBN 0-939481-46-4

Library of Congress Cataloging-in-Publication Data

```
Knopfhart, Alfred.
    [Dressur von A-S.  English]
    Dressage : a guidebook for the road to success / Alfred Knopfhart.
        p.   cm. -- (The Masters of horsemanship series ; bk. 1)
    ISBN 0-939481-46-4
    1. Dressage.  I.   Title. II Series.
SF309.5.K5713   1996                                    96-9489
798.2'3--dc20                                              CIP
```

Contents

Foreword

The first edition of this concentrated guide for schooling horses and riders from first level through Grand Prix came out in 1985. I have been gratified by the many positive reactions from dressage riders and trainers received by the four editions over ten years.

The fourth edition, revised, expanded and updated, and including the accurate and thoughtful drawings of Marianne Merz, met the interest of Half Halt Press, the prominent publisher of books on dressage and the horse. The result is this first English-language edition.

From the first day of our contact I felt my book was in the best hands and experience has proved that I was right. So I gladly take this occasion for a warm and cordial "thank you very much" to Elizabeth Carnes, the publisher, and to the translators who mastered a difficult task. I would also like to thank the staff for their efficient work and kind cooperation.

It is with great respect I have been following the highly remarkable international successes of dressage riders from the United States within the past ten years. Dressage is the fastest growing equestrian discipline in the United States and I know from my teaching tours in the States of the serious efforts of dressage riders there to gain knowledge of the discipline. Therefore, I would be very happy if my book might be of assistance and help for aspiring riders and thus could contribute to their success in classical dressage.

Alfred Knopfhart
February 1996
Laxenburg, Austria

Chapter 1

Tractability

What a world of meaning is behind the simple word *tractability*! It means everything in dressage, so let us examine it closely.

A correctly trained dressage horse is a perfectly obedient horse that allows his rider to sit easily to all gaits. He is not necessarily a horse with enormous impulsion and superb natural movement; in fact, it is often the case that a horse generously endowed by nature in these respects is insufficiently tractable to satisfy the above criterion.

The first three collective marks at the bottom of the competition test sheet concern the performance of the horse. The first two specifically refer to gaits and impulsion; related to the first two, the third mark is for submission and is, in effect, an assessment of what I am referring to as the "tractability" of the horse. It is stated, in brackets, that submission implies "attention and confidence, harmony, lightness and ease of the movements, acceptance of the bit and lightness of the forehand," all these being of course the essential elements of tractability.

A horse can be trained like a poodle to execute certain movements in obedience to commands and yet still may not be tractable. As one expert put it: "he does everything but nothing correctly."

A properly trained dressage horse moves easily and spontaneously, without having to be constantly urged on by his rider. In changes of direction and on curved lines like corners, he feels supple and in absolute control of his equilibrium. He executes all transitions smoothly. He is light in the hand and allows the rider to sit easily. In one word, all this amounts to *tractability*.

Is it possible for the dressage judge to gauge exactly how tractable a horse is? Certainly not, just on the basis of accurate execution of the movements of the test. At best, the accuracy in execution of some of the movements gives an inkling of tractability but the accuracy in execution of movements is not sufficient proof.

A horse that reels off the movements of a test like a child reciting a multiplication table can give a very rough ride. This is usually because he has at some time been forcibly compressed into an outline that caused him acute discomfort or because he has been made to perform movements for which his strength was inadequate, or because perhaps the rider habitually "pushes" with the seat bones or uses a loading seat effect ineptly. Consequently, the horse has progressively become stiffer, more uncomfortable, resistant and dispirited until, in the end, he resignedly does all he is told to do without ever having learned to flex his haunches and thus protect the rider against unpleasant jolting.

The rider has, in fact, obtained the very opposite of the stated aims of dressage training and should not be surprised to earn only faint praise for that performance.

A misconception in dressage very much exists nowadays, especially in so-called dressage-specialists' training establishments, where horses are drilled day after day to become conversant with one movement after another, yet are never rationally and progressively gymnastically exercised to enable them to execute those movements with the ease which should be shown in the tests. It is in those places that one finds, for example, horses that can do flying changes a *tempo* but are incapable of executing a simple change or a counter-canter, or can do a sort of passage but cannot move correctly at a collected trot. It is in those establishments that one sees riders who sit proudly to a piaffe on a specially trained horse (by no means a difficult feat) but who are incapable of getting a horse to rein back correctly or to step regularly in a half-pirouette, who are too frightened to trot over cavaletti, and almost fall off in an extended trot (if they ever venture to let the horse extend himself).

I am not exaggerating; this is born out by many witnesses. Offering this false dressage training may show good business sense and play to the ego of some riders but proper dressage, based on long established principles and sound methods, is something completely different.

Now back to the subject of "tractability" (Figure 1). If one assumes that a tractable horse moves so fluently in freely maintained self-carriage that the rider (presuming of course that the rider has learned to sit correctly) can maintain without difficulty a vertical and supple posture in all gaits, it follows that tractability can to a large extent be judged on the evidence of the rider's seat.

If a horse jolts his rider at every step of a medium trot, or stiffens his hind joints in the downward transitions, causing the rider to lean backward to offset the effect of inertia, the horse cannot be judged to be sufficiently tractable.

An important indication of tractability is the pliancy of the dorsal spine of the horse, pliancy that is the result of suppling exercises practiced daily for a number of years. On curved lines, through corners and in the two track movements, the horse must appear to bend from

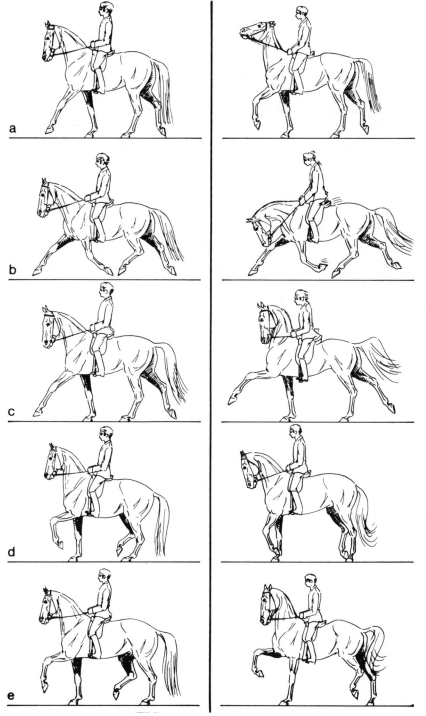

Figure 1: *Left column: Outward signs of tractability. Right column: Signs of insufficient tractability.* **a** = *Walk;* **b** = *Trot;* **c** = *Canter;* **d** = *Piaffe;* **e** = *Passage*

head to tail without resistance, seemingly of his own volition, and as easily to one side as to the other. He willingly consents to changes of flexion (the lateral flexion of the poll) without altering the regularity of his steps or stiffening his back and hind legs.

Moreover, a tractable horse yields as readily to the left or the right aids of reins and legs. This means not only that he obeys without hesitation the half halts or the full halt, but also that he complies equally with the forward, or forward and lateral, driving effects of either leg and executes the most difficult movements to both sides seemingly with equal facility.

It is, however, by the general manner of moving that the horse's tractability is most easily assessed. Tractable horses move with grace, with a spring in their steps, and almost noiselessly. They give the impression that they actually enjoy working. They can be collected easily, to a degree commensurate with their physical and mental development. The joints of the hind legs, compressed by the added load of the rider, flex and extend elastically, dampening the shocks of locomotion and thus protecting the rider against any jolting. As a result, again, it is the ease with which the rider sits to the movement that enables the judge to assess the correct activity of the back and hind leg muscles of the horse.

Chapter 2

Suppling and Collecting

Dressage exercises are divided into two principal categories: the exercises that are intended to supple, or loosen, muscles, and those that are designed to develop the strength of all the muscles involved in the collected gaits. All methods must first promote suppling since it is only when and if he is unconstrained that a horse can move correctly at the collected gaits.

The more advanced the horse is, the easier it should be to get him to loosen up. Unfortunately, the reverse is only too often the case: tenseness is frequently the consequence of execution of more difficult movements. If this tenseness is not immediately felt by the rider and promptly counteracted, it can become habitual. To avoid this risk the rider must be conversant with all suppling techniques and in the course of every lesson must remain attentive to signs of tenseness and frequently verify the state of suppleness of the horse.

The signs of suppleness are:

- regular, forward movement without any hesitation,
- activity of the back,
- flexibility of the poll,
- relaxed chewing of the bit and equal submission to the right and left hand,
- equal lateral suppleness,
- smoothness in the changes of flexion,
- the tilting of the crest towards the inside,
- calm lengthening of the reins by chewing the bit when the rider yields the contact.
- willingness to go forward on a loose rein,
- occasional snorting.

Deficiency in any of the above conditions indicates a certain degree of tenseness.

The following quotes are from highly respected authors of books about dressage.

"All horses, especially those suffering from some pain in the back or that tense up in certain situations, relax more readily if they are ridden in position instead of being held straight. The rider positions the horse inwards by tactfully acting with the inside rein and simultaneously yielding with the outside hand. In response, after a very short while most horses will allow themselves to be positioned to the inside.

The rider must ascertain to which rein the horse flexes its head with least difficulty; he can do this for example by changing the rein on a circle, executing a volte (on one track) in the opposite direction; if the horse does not offer the inside flexion of its head fairly soon to one hand, the rein is again changed back to the original circle. If the large circle does not induce flexion, one can try to obtain it on the volte. The change from flexion right to left, and vice versa is also helpful — the most important rule, at this stage of training, is to facilitate the flexion by yielding generously with the outside rein.

Once flexion is easily obtained, the inside hand must passively preserve the contact just making sure that the correct inside position is not lost. Should this happen - even for the shortest moment — a difficult lesson must cease immediately and position be restored by loosening exercises.

If the rider constantly invites the horse to go up to the outside rein by repeatedly advancing his outside hand, the outside muscle of the top of the neck will allow themselves to be stretched. Eventually the horse will adopt the correct inward position at the wish of the rider whenever the rider allows it to stretch the outside rein.

Provided that the rider never loses patience, the horse progressively establishes the habit of going up to the bit by relaxing the top muscles of the neck. The lengthening of the top muscles of the neck is essential to the establishment by the horse of even contact on both reins. The importance of active forward movement must, of course, never be forgotten and the horse may repeatedly have to be encouraged by the rider's legs to go up to the bit. Contraction of the muscles of the tongue, jaw, neck, back and hindquarters has to be overcome by sending the horse forwards at a rhythmical but energetic working trot, at a faster pace than it would offer of its own accord. It should become gradually easier to get the horse to loosen-up, to submit to the aids of legs, hands and seat and to move in horizontal equilibrium.

Momentary success has to be confirmed. Time after time the horse will have to be induced again to lengthen the top muscles of its neck until it realizes how pleasant it is to move in an unconstrained manner. Gradually its steps will become quieter and longer. Its back will start to swing, the muscles of either side in turn contracting and relaxing regularly instead of being held tight. When it feels the assistance to its equilibrium of the moderate tension of the reins which results from active and efficient forward movement, not only does it start to chew the bit, but it also flexes at the poll and its hindquarters start to take over some of the weight that was hampering the movements of its forelegs; it unresistingly allows itself to be lightened in front. Looseness is therefore an essential preparation of collection.

Author unknown, *Working Young Horses on the Snaffle:*

"When the horse is ridden on a circle, to preserve its equilibrium it has to engage its inside hind under the load and drive itself forward by swinging its outside hind energetically. To enable it to remain on the circle, it also has to reach out with its inside fore. A young horse that lacks sufficient strength in the hindquarters to support weight will overload its inside shoulder and consequently will progressively reduce the size of the circle.

To prevent this, the effect of the rider's aids must principally be to enlarge the circle. When the horse yields obediently to the inside rein, it comes again the outside rein which limits the flexion of the neck; submission to the inside rein puts the horse on the outside aids.

The inside aids must be the predominant ones until centrifugal force drives the horse onto the larger circle. It then comes up against the controlling outside aids which must prevent it from leaving the circle at a tangent. Once the horse maintains its equilibrium easily on the circle, the aids imperceptibly become more like the aids for travers than the aids for shoulder-in.

In the process, the moment soon occurs when the horse inflexes its head spontaneously when the rider advances his outside hand. Guidance then becomes the function of the outside hand. The horse chews the bit on the outside rein and the contact with the inside hand feels very soft (Figure 2).

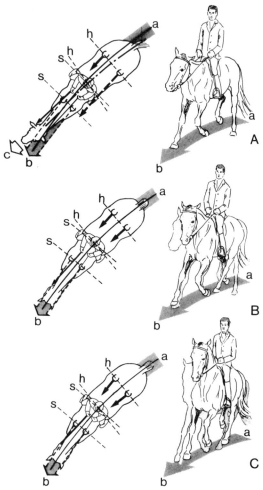

Figure 2: *Suppling and collecting exercises on the circle.* **A** = *Stiff, laterally inflexible horse;* **B** = *Supple, bending horse;* **C** = *Beginning of collection.* **h** = *Hips of horse, hips of rider;* **s** = *Shoulders of horse, shoulders of rider;* **a, b** = *Longitudinal axis.*

"The horse will especially attempt to avoid engaging its inside hind, using it rather as a buttress to help it resist better the bend of the constitutionally stiffer parts of its body. It is principally on this inside hind that the rider must concentrate his attention; he must use his inside leg or spur to cause the inside hind to step not only further forward but also closer to the line of action of the outside hind; the inside hind thus is obliged to support the weight of the mass and to flex all its joints. This seemingly simple prescription is the foundation of the whole process of dressage right up to the most advanced stage. It prepares the much valued shoulder-in; or rather one can say that it is the foundation of the shoulder-in. Neither gaits nor bending can be properly developed if the inside hind does not engage properly and all resistances of the horse, without exception, can be traced back to disregard of this principle.

Many horses are quite clever at tricking the rider by bending their neck in front of the withers; they then avoid the engagement and loading of the inside hind by placing it beside the trace of the inside fore; however they cannot outwit the good rider who recognizes the evasion partly because of the slackness of the inside rein, but mainly because he feels himself sliding to the outside; he will then have to exaggerate the displacement of his weight to the inside and thereby force the horse to tread under the mass with its inside hind and flex its inside haunch. The energetic use of the forward and sideways impelling aids of whip and spur on circles of an appropriate radius and the speed of the pace are the only effective ways of countering the resistance and teaching the horse respect for the inside leg.

When equal contact and flexion of the head to both sides can be easily obtained, the rein effects will extend to the hind limbs. Moreover, when equal tension of the reins is the result of the horse's submission to the aids, the tension feels lighter in the hand when the forehand is elevated and more firmly in the hand at the extended gaits. This is proof of the firm connection established between the neck and the back which allows an elevation of the forehand based on engaged and supporting hindquarters.

Burkner, *A Lifetime in the Saddle:*

". . .in N's method of teaching riders to put the horse on the outside rein to both hands, he divides the ride so that one section works on a circle to the right hand and the other on a circle to the left hand. The horses, positioned inward, are urged on to canter by the energetic use of the rider's inside leg. This has the effect of easing the tension on the inside rein and of maintaining the position of the horse by getting it to stretch the outside rein. When this results is achieved, the rides change hand. As a result of this work, the shortened muscles of one side are naturally obliged to be elongated. After approximately half-an-hour of this work, the two rides are remerged into one and, to prove the effectiveness of the exercise, the whole ride goes large, with the distance between each horse exactly maintained, at a medium trot. All horses should stretch both reins equally and show considerable impulsion. Every rider ought to be able to feel the slightest sign of lateral stiffness and unequal tension of reins. Work on the circle in two rides moving in opposite direction is then resumed, with those horses still evidencing an uneven tension of reins going in the direction designed to counter their resistance. This method of promoting suppleness, allowing constant observation by the teacher of the seat and aids of each rider, is extremely beneficial to the education of the horse and rider."

The suppling process is very precisely described in the above concurring texts. It can be developed through special exercises such as the turn on the forehand, leg-yielding, repeated transitions from working trot to medium canter, and trotting over cavaletti.

The essential thing in all this work is to put the horse on the outside aids. The outside rein must eventually assume the guiding role while the inside rein, together of course with the outside leg, just maintains the degree of general bend and, therefore, the radius of the turns and circles. It is with the outside rein that the forehand is placed in front of the hindquarters and the driving force of the hind legs can then work in the direction of the center of gravity. The propulsive power of the hind limbs thus becomes fully effective. One can then begin to work on the collected gaits, with care to preserve the fluency achieved by the suppling work and with due regard to the age, conformation and stage of education of the horse.

Chapter 3

Turns and Curves

Included in these lessons are all changes of direction, shallow loops, circles, and right-angled changes of direction as when riding through the corners of the school. They are considered together, but there are special points to each which I will go into later. It may appear so simple to change direction in the course of forward movement as to hardly deserve the expenditure of more than a few words, but the subject is more complex than it may seem. A number of unsuspected but important difficulties are apt to crop up in those apparently simple movements that can seriously impede subsequent progress. This goes for both horse and rider, and a rider who doubts this fact should set for her or himself a test: by riding through the corner of the school and turning precisely onto the centerline facing C. The rider will quickly find out that it is not such an easy matter.

Since a horse is incapable of bending his body at a right angle to execute a turn, he is obliged to round off the corner of right-angled changes of direction by executing them as a quarter-circle. To remain exactly on the track, he has to bend to the same degree as the curvature of the quarter-circle.

The deeper one rides through the corner, the smaller the diameter of the circle, the greater the bend required and the more supple the horse must be. However, the "correct" execution of turns will be explained later.

The introductory remarks are intended to show that suppling exercises, like most of the exercises of the "low school" (at the lower levels), have a dual purpose: they must facilitate changes of direction and they must develop the lateral flexibility of the rib cage. We will consider them solely from the latter point of view and see how their correct execution develops a horse's suppleness.

All textbooks of horsemanship explain rather tersely how turns have to be executed and which aids to employ. It is unnecessary to repeat here the rules that can be read in any one of those manuals. However, the ancient rules of the classical school of riding (or of other schools) sometimes have had to be slightly amended. For instance, it used to be stated that the radius of a quarter-circle was equal to three strides of the walk; this has now been changed to three meters.

Three strides infers a quarter of a circle of a diameter of 4.80 meters, and much more incurvation than a quarter of a circle with a diameter of six meters.

The latter still requires an extreme degree of suppleness ("bend of the third degree"). At the very beginning of his dressage training, the most a horse can achieve is a bend of the "first degree," corresponding to the curvature of a 20 m circle. By the time the horse is considered ready to compete at training and first level, the horse ought to be able to bend in a corner to a degree corresponding to the curvature of a 10 m to 7 m volte; it follows that a bend of the third degree, corresponding to the curvature of a volte of a diameter of 6 m (formerly 4.80 m) is possible only for a horse of advanced (second to third) level (Figure 3).

Therefore, to be able to execute correctly the changes of direction on one track required in dressage tests, a horse has to be well advanced in his education and a considerable degree of suppleness has to be attained.

Every rider who has trained young horses will have learned through experience that the unaccustomed presence on his back of a rider, no matter how light the latter may be, has a seriously unbalancing effect on the horse even on a straight track along the wall of the school. The unbalancing effect of the weight of the rider is considerably increased when direction has to be changed at the end of the long side. Therefore, during the course of the first weeks of schooling, one should forget the rules which have to be respected at a later stage regarding position, transitions, two tracks movements, etc.; one must ride on as straight a course as possible. But even in a large arena and in the course of the first lessons, the straight long side eventually comes to an end and the direction has to be changed at least four times—that is if one wants to remain in the arena!

Although the horse should be allowed at this stage to avail himself of the undeniable balancing aid of the wall and to round the corners as much as possible, one can feel the awkwardness with which a completely untrained horse, even a calm one that has had a thorough preparation by work on the lunge, executes the turn. Even if the horse has managed to preserve a straight course and an even speed along the wall of the long side, making him turn across the arena, away from the wall, at this stage would be an adventure with unpredictable results. It is wise not to risk it before the horse has been worked for long enough at the trot to get him to relax, lower his neck and find a balancing aid in the tension of reins, that is, before he has learned to understand and obey the simple inside flexing leg and rein aids of the rider in the corners and to maintain a relatively steady speed when changing direction.

Even then, it is rare that the horse will react just as the rider wishes when first asked to turn across the arena. He may slow down or

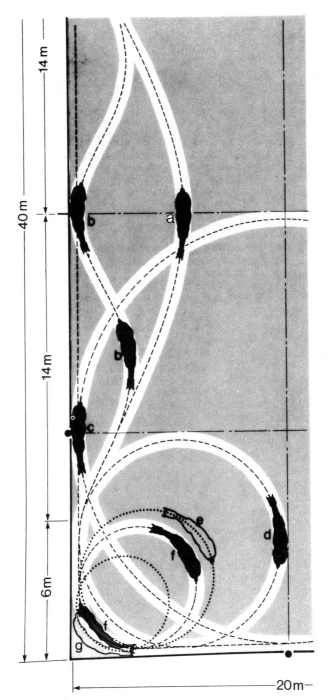

Figure 3: *Various degrees of difficulty in obtaining spinal flexion on one track (in a 20 x 40 m arena).* **a**. *Shallow loop;* **b**. *Double loop;* **c**. *20 m circle;* **d**. *10 m volte;* **e**. *7 m volte;* **f**. *6 m volte;* **g**. *5 m volte (formerly 6 steps of 80 cm).*

speed up or fail to get on the line of the indicated course. He may even be reluctant to turn away from the wall and, if forced to do so, will turn suddenly by throwing out the hindquarters.

What a contrast with the changes of direction of the well-trained, light-footed, supple horse! His speed, carriage and bend remain constant as he follows all the correct tracks of the figures with equal impulsion and expressiveness in all the gaits.

With the false hope of saving time, there are many riders who shrug off the necessity of developing the suppleness of their horse by work on circles and fractions of circles, believing that the result will be achieved automatically in the course of further dressage training. This is not the case. On the contrary: the production of a degree of bend corresponding precisely to the curve of a quarter of a circle is the basis of preservation of equilibrium in riding figures and, at a later stage, in lateral movements and all other exercises in which the correct bend is a condition of correct execution of a movement. Riders who disregard the importance of this stage of the horse's education, who tackle all difficulties of dressage at the same time or plan their program of training in reverse order ought not to be surprised if sooner or later they become "stuck." They then have to backtrack and realize that the short cuts have turned out to be a waste of time and effort.

"I cannot understand why my horse can do everything except a canter-pirouette" is a frequently heard lament. The horse may perhaps do everything, but how? He is probably incapable of preserving a collected canter as he turns the corners of the arena; and if he cannot do this, how can he do a volte, since a volte is simply an immediate succession of four corners which, like the pirouette, may frequently have to be performed on an inside track, away from the balancing aid of the wall? If a horse cannot do a volte on a single track, he will certainly not be able to do a volte on two tracks; and a pirouette (according to the definition by the FEI) is a volte on two tracks with a radius equal to the length of the horse.

There are many riders who have not mastered the knack of turning corners because they have underestimated the importance and difficulty of such an apparently simple thing and have foolishly skipped this particular lesson; they always experience difficulties in the execution of more advanced movements, all in fact based on the technique of turning the corners. Noting the frequently awkward execution of the more difficult movements in advanced tests, one of our foremost experts would say: "They cannot even ride a serpentine."

With unknown horses which are sent to us for training or correcting, after the suppling work one of our favorite exercises is the exact turning of corners at all the gaits. This is where so many horses and riders come unstuck. For centuries had the lesson not been found so valuable, indeed essential to the continuation of dressage work, the ground plan of the classical manege would have been elliptical instead of rectangular. The fact that an elliptical shape facilitates the work of horses and riders is proved by the hoof prints of the horses in most riding schools. The narrow arena has many disadvantages, but specifically for dressage training it has the advantage that the corners have to be turned more frequently and the difficulty this creates can be compounded by riding the half-arena. However, the width of a arena should never be less than 12 m as there must be room to lengthen the strides between corners.

If a rider and horse that have become stuck at some stage of their more or less advanced education come to you for help, after the horse has been properly suppled by appropriate exercises, you can start by marking out a 10 m square with two sides enclosed by the wall of the arena. The straight lines and the corners must be ridden so exactly that the horse can be ridden perfectly straight for a distance of 4 m on every side of the square and be made to go round the corners with correct bend (Figure 4).

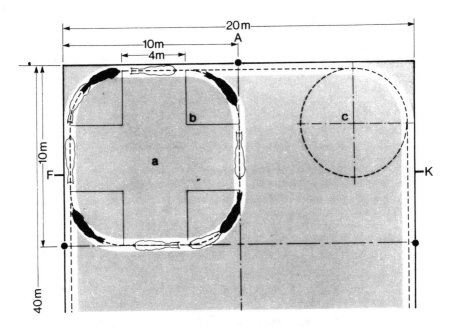

Figure 4: **a**. *Square volte of 10 m;* **b**. *Quarter section of a circle in the corner;* **c**. *Volte of 6 m.*

You will be able to gain useful insight into the rider's problems if you ask him to ride this square volte to both hands, first at walk, then at collected trot and canter. While executing the exercise, the horse should be able to preserve a regular rhythm and unchanging outline. There are always some riders who get annoyed and cannot understand why they should bother to teach their horse to do this simple exercise or similar ones correctly and you will not be able to help them. Success always eludes those who are not prepared to try.

If one's aim is simply to ride more or less correctly in open country, inability to ride tight corners in perfect equilibrium is of little importance. There are, however, always days when the weather compels one to ride inside—or to let the horse stand in the stall for a day or two. But an intractable horse will always find the most spacious of arenas too small and so it is understandable that the rider should give up the doubtful pleasure of struggling with an unwieldy animal in this confined, uninspiring environment. The best use he can think of making of it is as a sheltered place in which to conduct at the walk on the inside track a quiet gossip on horseback!

It is undeniable that the correct riding of curved lines is an important index of the tractability of a horse and also one of the best means of developing it. As a matter of interest, one can count the number of times turns must have to be executed in dressage tests in comparison with other movements. It is now time to analyze the elements of their correct execution.

As all students of equitation know, each leg, rein and seat bone has a particular role to play. The backward displacement of outside knee and lower leg by no more than a hands width behind the normal position at the girth, the forward position of inside hip and outside shoulder in the turns are essential elements of a good seat. In fact, the "turning seat," "bending seat," or whatever it may be called in languages (other than German), requires a high degree of suppleness in the torso, of balance and independence of knee grip, and reins that have to be acquired by conscientious and often tiresome work. But a rider who has to rely for security on grip and reins cannot hope to succeed in teaching a horse to bend correctly, that is, evenly from head to tail.

It must be said that this seat demands a muscular adaptation and that initially the necessary suppling and lengthening of the muscles of the inner surface of the thighs is not entirely painless. However, once this deep seat becomes established, it is a very comfortable one and provides the rider with maximum effectiveness in all the exercises designed to promote the suppleness of the horse's spine and rib cage (Figure 5).

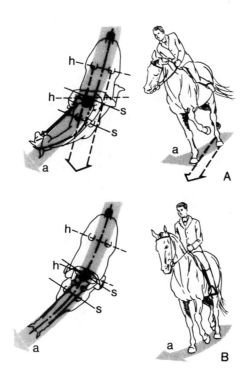

Figure 5: *The bending or turning seat.* **A** = *Exaggerated;* **B** = *Correct.* **a** = *Longitudinal axis;* **h** = *Horse's hips, rider's hips;* **s** = *Horse's shoulders, rider's shoulders.*

The majority of riders nowadays sit in the way which they find most comfortable and dismiss the classical seat, (the *sine qua non* of effective influence in dressage schooling of horses), as an outmoded thing that can be acquired only at the cost of tedious practice. Bringing the lower leg back, sometimes almost horizontal, and thereby lifting up the outside thigh and knee, is a totally ineffectual way of trying to get a horse to bend; it is a merely useless exaggeration of only one of the aids needed. The classical seat is absolutely essential for the dressage trainer; it can be acquired only under the guidance of a genuine teacher. But a rider who has established it will, in the course of time, be capable of education his own horses to bend correctly and to perform all the other exercises based on the fundamental one of turning corners correctly. If the rider fails to establish this seat, it is the horse that will impose upon the rider whatever position the horse finds less inconvenient, he will evade the action of the annoying position of the outside leg simply by pushing it forward, and he will continue to avoid flexing the joints of the inside haunch, continuing to make the rider slide to the outside instead of letting him sit softly on his inside seat bone. The horse will either take the turns as a succession of straight lines or will throw his shoulders into the turn by bending his neck the wrong way.

It is a fact that there are many riders who are wrongly positioned in turns, on circles and voltes and whose outside leg is further forward than their inside one. I do not propose to analyze the causes of this phenomenon: suffice it to say that for reasons sufficiently explained, correct turns, circles or serpentines are impossible if the rider does not put his weight on his inside seat bone and he ought not to be surprised to lose many marks in a dressage test on this account.

Selective breeding has put on the market today a large number of horses with naturally good movement, with a conformation that facilitates safe equilibrium and with a favorable temperament that, after only a few weeks of familiarization with the weight of the rider and of learning to respond to elementary aids of legs and reins, could be well presented in novice dressage tests — were it not for the turns and the riding of circles, turns and serpentines. A naturally straight horse, that is, one that is laterally flexible to the same degree to both hands, has not yet been born. Equal suppleness in both directions is a result of education of the horse by the rider and this obviously takes time. While it requires very little skill on the part of the rider to allow a horse with natural aptitude to extend to medium trot, riding correctly a change of direction or a volte is a different thing and demonstrates better than a few lengthened strides—however impressive they may be—the dexterity of the horse and the ability of the rider.

It is for the purpose of schooling the horse to change direction without altering his equilibrium that riding halls and rings are rectangular. The walls help one considerably to ride the horse straight before and after the turns. Touching the points marking the end and the beginning of the straight lines helps one to concentrate on executing the turning of corners in the shape of a quarter-circumference of a circle. The difficulty in correct execution of corners and curves, which involves increased flexion of the joints of the inside haunch, and overall bend incite the horse to seek a variety of ways of avoiding effort. Turning his croup outward allows the horse to evade bending; placing the inside hind sideways or falling out on the outside shoulder obviates the necessity of flexing the inside joints; the horse may also cut the corner, bend the neck only, decrease or increase the speed, or deviate outward from the straight line before the turn so as to provide himself with room to change direction on a wider arc of a circle. These common evasions or any other must all be scrupulously corrected.

When they occur on the outside track despite the limitations imposed by the presence of walls, one can easily imagine how much more difficult it is to change direction with precision when riding on an inside track. It requires much practice and a trained eye to ride a precise volte or fraction of one correctly at the trot or canter without the optical aids of the markers on the walls.

In the early stages of schooling one is strongly advised to pay great attention to the correctness of the turns and never let the horse find the easy way out of the difficulty. When correct turns can be executed easily on the outside track on both hands at all three gaits and the horse is ready for the collected gaits, all changes of direction at any place in the arena will have to be ridden with the same careful attention to correct bend.

Alternately riding straight lines and correct turns (of a radius appropriate to the stage of training of the horse) at an absolutely regular rhythm and with unaltering steadiness of neck carriage, is an incomparable way of producing a supple, tractable horse, perfectly obedient to the aids of leg, weight and reins.

For a dedicated horseman, the result is surely worth the effort.

Chapter 4

Circles and Voltes

Circles and voltes are the continuation of the work on turns discussed in the previous chapter. All the principles stated in that chapter apply to the riding of these figures which are just a further practical application of the same principles. There are, however, certain difficulties inherent in the riding of complete circles rather than sections of circles.

Voltes and circles alike are completely round figures, though of different diameters. However, for the sake of clarity, we must examine first the criteria of correct execution of circles, and later those relevant to the riding of voltes.

The FEI *Rules For Dressage* state that a volte is a circle of six meters diameter. If the diameter is greater, the word circle should be used, and its diameter must be stated.

If no indication of the dimension of the circle is indicated, it is assumed that it is the largest one that can be contained within the bounds of the arena (and there are good reasons why an arena ought to measure no more than 20 and no less than 12 meters across).

A volte of six meters is the smallest circle that can be executed on one track without deterioration of the regularity of the gait, and it demands an advanced degree of education. In elementary and medium tests the smallest circles prescribed will be of seven to eight meters in diameter. Such circles can be called voltes, of a stated size, and so can the figure eight on the short side of the ring, which consists of two 10 meter circles.

It has already been said that it is impossible to ride turns correctly if one has not mastered the "bending" or "turning" seat. It is the only means of teaching a horse to bend in turns and on any circle or fraction of a circle.

It should be unnecessary to explain what a bending seat is. One cannot have had any education in horsemanship if one does not know in theory the combination of aids of which it consists; it is described in every manual of horsemanship. Nevertheless, it may take years of painstaking riding education to perfect the posture that allows the necessary suppleness, but one cannot hope to teach a horse to bend correctly to both hands in all three gaits on turns, corners, circles and voltes if one has not mastered this seat. This is why so many riders who venture too soon to appear in public seem competent enough on the straight but give one the impression of being inept or helpless on circles and even more so on voltes.

It is also why work on circles so often fails to produce the intended result. A rider who cannot assume a bending seat when necessary, even after months of so-called work on circles, will not succeed in producing a more supple horse, while another may obtain this result within a relatively short time. This is one more example of the aptness of the old proverb that in the art of horsemanship, what matters is not so much "what" to do as "how" to do it.

In contrast with the turn on the haunches, circles and voltes do not really serve a practical purpose (though in the past voltes were considered essential to victory in had-to-hand combat).

In modern dressage, however, they remain valuable but only as a means to an end. Dressage riders or trainers who understand their purpose may well earn pitying looks from those who think that there are more expedient ways of producing the same result than "endless going round in circles." Let the ignorant sneer, but riders who are just plain lazy have no right to ridicule those who are prepared to work intelligently.

Shrugging his shoulders at the chronic mockers, the educated horseman will not only change speed and gait with astuteness, but will also use straight or circular lines as necessary, riding straight out of a circle as soon as he feels that he has achieved his aim on the circle, and on the straight proving the result hopefully attained by work on the circle.

He knows that work on circles has more than one object:

* it is the quickest way of getting a horse supple;

* it is the best way of producing first degree bending and, consequently, increased loading and flexion of the inside hock in preparation of collected work and flexion of the haunches:

* it promotes suppleness and agility;

* it helps to correct the one-sidedness common to all horses much more easily than does riding on the straight;

* it has a strong calming effect on excitable horses;

* last but not least, it advances the education of the rider as well as that of the horse (Figure 6).

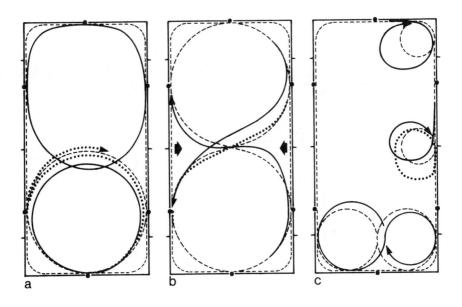

Figure 6: *Precision in the work on circles.* ------ = *Trace of correctly executed circle or fraction of a circle;* ____ = *Inaccurate figure;* .... = *Inaccurate figure. Appropriate position of teacher shown by thick arrows;* a = *Circle;* b = *Change of hand out of the circle;* c = *Voltes and figure of eight on the short side of the arena.*

The intended effect of working on circles can be achieved only on condition that the correct line of the circle is followed as accurately as possible, but it is difficult to convince riders of the importance of accuracy. Many want quick and easy results and soon lose heart when they discover that riding a correct circle is not as simple a matter as it seems. We have been taught at school that all points of a circle are equidistant from the center point. However, the so-called circles ridden on horseback frequently bear only some vague resemblance to that geometrical figure. This would not matter terribly (and is unavoidable even for a good rider on an imperfectly schooled horse) if at least an attempt at accuracy were made, but this is rarely the case and the majority of riders are completely unperturbed when their horse cuts corners or deviates from the correct shape of a circle by several meters. They are like musicians who do not realize that they have hit a wrong note or, worse still, do not care about the ugliness of the resulting sound.

But why does the instructor not set them straight? The answer is simply that there is no instructor to be seen or heard. So many people believe that they can teach themselves and educate their horses without having to pay for competent tuition, especially those who most need it.

Every horse will discover some way of avoiding what he feels to be the unnecessary effort of flexing his spine correctly if his rider is inattentive. This is surely more a sign of intelligence than of cussedness on the horse's part. In the same circumstances, humans would not behave differently.

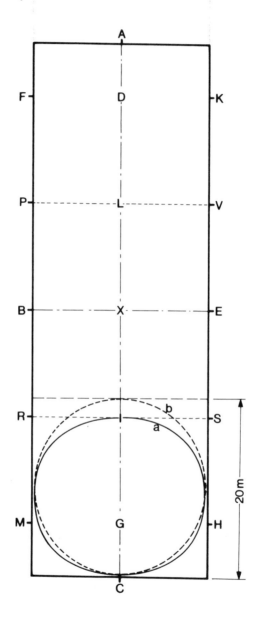

Figure 7: *Precise riding on a twenty meter circle.* **a** = *Faulty;* **b** = *Correct.*

In a twenty by sixty meter arena, one frequently observes during the course of the test that riders seem to think that the line P - V or R - S indicates the limits of the circle. This is not so. This line is only eighteen meters from the short side, therefore, two more meters short of the diameter of twenty meters imposed by the standard width of the arena (Figure 7).

Some may object that this is an insignificant detail. Even riders with many years of experience of dressage competitions are unaware of this fact and use those markers as optical aids when they are required to execute a twenty meter circle. One cannot therefore say that the detail is insignificant.

A perfect twenty meter circle cannot be executed with a horse that is too stiff to bend to the circumference of the circle. An untrained horse can only at best execute the exercise as a series of short lines and obtuse angles; the result is a polygon rather than a circle. There are many horses, especially those with an unfavorable conformation, that show considerable reluctance to maintain an overall bend for any length of time. One should never, of course, provoke a battle; the best, or even only, way of advancing a young horse's dressage education without frequent setbacks is to work him correctly on circles of progressively reduced diameter. All horses will naturally try various evasions, especially at the beginning of training. Since the education of horses must always be progressive, the first thing to achieve is control of the inside hind by riding on a fairly large circle with special activity of one's inside leg. The way to put the horse on the diagonal aids and neutralize resistance to the inside rein is to drive him forward with the inside leg to the outside hand. In all turns, it is the inside hind that has to do most of the work and the majority of horses will attempt to place it beside the trace of the outside fore to avoid the effort of supporting weight. The rider's inside leg must continually request the horses's inside hind foot to step in the track of the inside fore. Timely prevention of the horse's usual evasion of effort demands on the part of the rider considerable effectiveness.

When the rider has mastered the inner side (a fact that should be verified by an observer on the ground) and feels the horse come up to the outside aids (as a consequence of obedience to the inside aids), the rider must then prevent the turning out of the outside hind. To this purpose it is necessary to position the outside leg somewhat behind its normal place at the girth (even at the rising trot) and to use the outside rein upon which the horse will now put a positive tension. The outside rein may have to assist the guarding outside leg by putting the horse's shoulders in front of the outside hind.

Bending of the first degree can be considered achieved when the horse responds satisfactorily to those aids and the rider has obtained control of both sides. Riding straight along the walls of the arena is advisable in the case of horses that show a tendency to deviate outwards with the outside hind and are not yet sufficiently obedient to the outside leg. The wall assists the outside leg, but it must not of course be allowed to become a substitute for the leg. On circles, in corners and in changes of hand, it is the outside rein that must fulfill the role of the wall.

One can say that a horse is on the aids and correctly bent on the large circle when he applies an even tension to both reins, when both hind feet tread in the tracks of the forefeet, when the crest tips over to the inside, and when the horse maintains the bend when the rider surrenders the contact with the inside rein.

One should not, however, expect the horse to maintain the bend on his own for any length of time. To keep him precisely on the line of the circle, the rider must remain extremely attentive and continuously, though imperceptibly, alternate between shoulder-in and travers-like aids according to the tendency of the horse to fall in or out from the prescribed line (Figure 8).

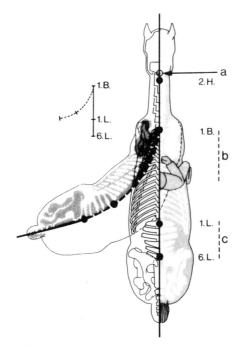

Figure 8: *Lateral suppleness of the vertebral column of the horse.* **1.B.** *Thoracic vertebrae;* 1.L. *and* 6 .L. *Lumbar vertebrae;* 2 .H. *Cervical vertebrae.* **a** = *Swivel joint (axis);* **b** = *Vertebrae forming the withers;* **c** = *Lumbar vertebrae (from* **Anatomy of the Domestic Dog** *by Nickel, Schummer & Seiferle).*

Fortunately, there are only three places where the horse can break the uniform bend of his vertebral column: at the poll (the axis), at the withers, and at the joint of the last thoracic and first lumbar vertebrae. If the neck is excessively bent, the horse will fall out on his outside shoulder or twist his poll. Remember, the rider controls the forehand with the reins. He controls the activity and the line of action of the hindquarters with his legs. Turning the hindquarters in is a particularly bad fault because it is not easily detected by the rider, but their turning out is easy to feel and must always be prevented by the outside rein and outside leg, and not by one aid alone. In very bad cases, one can position the horse outwards, but it is important to limit the outside position to the flexion of the head and to prevent bending of the neck in front of the withers. The outward position must never be maintained longer than necessary to achieve the intended result.

It should be noted that it is not unusual to see riders attempting to produce an inward or outward position by crossing a hand over to the opposite side of the withers. It would take too long to enumerate all the drawbacks of this serious fault. However, one of its most serious consequences is that on the side of the erring hand, that hind limb is then free to evade its weight supporting function. The invariable rule regarding the position of the hands is that each hand must always remain, not necessarily in one set place, but always on its own side of the horse's neck. It is totally illogical to attempt to produce a head position to the right with a rein effect towards the left, or vice versa. Yet there are always riders who think that they know better and ignore this inviolable prescription of classical horsemanship; it is surprising that their attempts to straighten the horse are doomed to failure.

The teacher must place himself outside the circle to enable him to observe the seat and the aids of the rider from all sides, as well as the tracks of the horse's hooves. It is only from this position that he can judge whether work on the circle produces the intended results in both directions. He must also be able to note whether the horse changes flexion smoothly in the changes of direction. For the latter purpose, the most appropriate figures are the changes of hand "away from the circle," the figure eight on the short side, and serpentines.

All points of a circle are, of course, equidistant from the center point. In addition, the appropriate place for the execution of an exercise is not a matter for indifference since in an arena a circle has a "closed" and an "open" side (except circles that are executed in the middle of the school). A beginner will unfailingly choose the wrong place and the wrong moment to start the exercise. It is the duty of the teacher to explain to the pupil how best he can utilize work on the circle by selecting the most appropriate place. For example, the first stages of educating horse or rider to canter with the inside lead are much facilitated if the aids are given at the end of a long side, when the walls and the short side form a helpful boundary which to a considerable extent prevents a mere hurrying of the trot.

In cases when the rider cannot prevent the horse deviating outward from the circle on the open side, a useful exercise is the "square," with one of its sides against the wall of the short side of the arena. This figure seems to help pupils to get a better understanding of the aids for circling. After repeated rounding of the corners of the square, the result is usually a passable circle.

To conclude the theme of the twenty meter circle, I offer another piece of advice for the benefit of the advanced rider. In more advanced education, work on the circle on two tracks is a good way of improving the suppleness and agility of many horses. On straight lines, whether one rides, for example, travers or renvers right, makes no difference. It can be called one or the other according to what one decides is the line to follow and from the point of view of the horse the movements are the same. However, on curved lines and especially on the circle the main

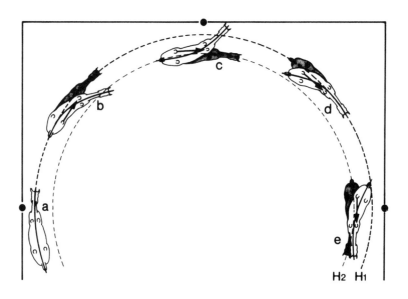

Figure 9: *Two track work on the circle.* **H 1** = *Outer track ;* **H 2** = *Inner track;* **a** = *On the circle;* **b** = *Shoulder-in;* **c** = *Counter shoulder-in;* **d** = *Travers;* **e** = *Renvers.*

differences are very evident. Counter shoulder-in and travers have a greater collecting effect than shoulder-in since the hindquarters, having to move on a smaller circle than the shoulders, must support the weight more. Conversely, if renvers is performed on the circle it is difficult to sufficiently load the hindquarters, which are then on the outer circumference, and therefore also difficult to maintain collection (Figure 9).

Everything that has been said about work on the circle applies without exception to the execution of voltes. There are some additional details however. For example, although the volte today is usually a circular figure, in de la Gueriniere's time in France the volte was exclusively in the form of a square. It was always ridden on two tracks for the purpose of developing the travers, renvers or the pirouettes. The word comes from the Italian (voltea=circle) and while in Italy always indicated a circle, the French used to call the Italian Volte the *redoppio*.

The square volte on one track was also performed in the Germanic schools but for some unaccountable reason it is not favored there any longer. It has so many advantages that I think that it should not be dismissed with a mere mention. It is made up of four right angles; at first the sides are eight meters long and the corners are ridden as a quarter of a circle of a radius of precisely three meters. Thus each side presents the possibility of straightening the horse for just one length of his body. The figure must be executed with remarkable precision (read again the chapter on bends and turns).

A rider who has learned to execute the square volte correctly will certainly be able to perform a perfectly circular volte much more easily than another who has not had such training. Rounding the corners of the square volte a little more automatically produces a circle. However, the square volte is quite an exacting and beneficial exercise and there are not many riders capable of alternately straightening and bending their horse on such a small figure.

The special purpose of the volte is to produce greater bending (of the second or third degree depending on the radius), to increase the loading and flexion of the inside hind joints and develop the suppleness, handiness and submission of the horse.

Since the value of the exercise depends entirely on precise execution, it is advisable at the beginning to practice either the square volte or the circular one in a corner where the presence of two walls offers a convenient boundary. A horse that has been properly prepared by the correct execution of turns across the ring and in the corners should not find the exercise difficult. The difficulty can then be enhanced by executing the same figure on a radius that depends on the degree of education of the horse in the middle of the long or the short side of the arena. Both halves of the volte should be absolutely equal but unless the rider is extremely attentive, the horse will always make one half smaller or larger than the other.

The exercise is included in Intermediate II (volte right of 6 m diameter immediately followed by a volte left of the same diameter) and it is a stumbling block for many competitors. The speed and rhythm must be the same on both voltes; the horse's carriage and bend must be correct. He must also change flexion smoothly as he moves from one volte onto the other. Both voltes must be exactly the same size and perfectly circular, and the difficulty is compounded by the fact that they are to be executed in the middle of the arena.

A horse that has not been carefully prepared by methodical gymnastic training will not be capable of executing this figure correctly, and to obtain a high mark, even with a well-trained horse, the rider must be very attentive to the correctness of his aids. In fact, very few riders manage to get a mark better than a 6, especially from the side judges who are in this instance particularly well placed to compare both voltes.

Voltes and circles of varying diameters with corresponding degrees of bend play such an important role in the development of dressage horses that they should be a daily lesson for them, especially in combination with one or another of the lateral movements. In fact, they are so valuable a means of improving the tractability of all horses that they should be included in the training program of horses that are being trained for other riding disciplines. Riders rarely appreciate the importance and may not ride a volte or circle for weeks or even months and when the thought of doing so does occur to them, they usually fail to repeat the exercise when it has been performed incorrectly. It is as if they find relief in getting back to straight lines—which can never be long enough — and their interminable circuits of the whole school. But the good effects of voltes usually show themselves only after the execution of several of them, either in the same or another place. This is precisely stated in the "Guiding Principles" of the FEI: "The riding of voltes is especially conducive to the development of the agility and submissiveness of horses. It is therefore recommended that several voltes on the same place be executed consecutively."

The volte at the canter especially requires continual turning and skillful direction of the forehand with well-controlled leg action. Before rider and horse have become sufficiently proficient, it is easier and more advantageous to practice the exercise in the form of the "square volte," of ten meters to start with, rather than the circular volte.

Casually ask a number of riders how many springs (or "bounds") of a relatively collected canter a horse ought to put in on an eight meter volte, and you will be surprised at the variety of answers. Most riders will answer between four and eight springs. This reveals both an underestimation of the diameter of the circle and ignorance of the length of the springs in a collected canter. Now a volte of eight meters represents a circumference of 25.13 meters. This means that twelve springs of a length of approximately two meters, fourteen of a length of 1.75 m, sixteen of a length of 1.50 m will have to be made to complete the volte, presuming that this is a perfect volte of a constant diameter of 8 m.

Obviously, without the optical aids of markers, as for example in a large field, a rider's estimation of distance and his skillfulness would have to be remarkable to enable him to appraise correctly the size and accuracy of a volte. And the horse's is even worse!

Chapter 5

The Turn on the Forehand and Leg-Yielding

Leg-yielding, according to an extremely reliable author, cannot be described as a "lateral" movement because the horse in this movement has to "yield" to the outside leg of the rider (Figure 10). The head and neck of the horse are inflected outwards, the rider's inside leg is usually inoperative and the incorrectly flexed horse is forced to move sideways by the outside leg, with his nose against the wall of the arena. Regularity of footfalls and equilibrium deteriorate. Proper lateral movements, on the contrary, are simultaneously forward and sideways; in contrast, leg-yielding can only be described as irregular sideways movement. The horse is prevented from going forward by the presence of the wall. According to the aforementioned author, leg-yielding is definitely not a lesson to introduce into the curriculum for dressage horses.

The author is not the sole objector to the movement. So let us read what our presently accepted authority, the FEI, has to say on the subject, Article 411 of the *Rules for Dressage* states that:

Leg-yielding is a most important preparation for all lateral movements. It must be included in the program of education of the horse before it is ready to move in collection. Like the shoulder-in at a more advanced stage, leg-yielding is the best means of teaching a horse to loosen up, to move in a free, unconstrained manner, to develop free, elastic gaits and harmonious, light and easy movement.

Such total disagreement is very confusing for students of dressage. A reconciliation of views is possible, however, which is what I will now attempt to achieve.

The FEI clearly maintains that leg-yielding is a lateral movement. Article 411, Section 7 states: "The lateral movements include leg-yielding, shoulder-in, travers (head to the wall) renvers (croup to the wall) and travers (half-pass)."

This classification is not universally accepted. According to the traditional teaching of central Europe, the lateral movements are characterized by bending in the direction of the movement along with collection, and are means of improving suppleness and collection. The superficial resemblance of leg-yielding with the classical lateral movements resides in the forward-sideways movement, but the resemblance ceases there since the general bend of neck and body and

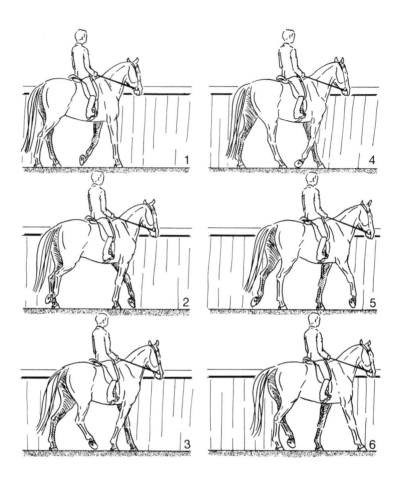

Figure 10: *On the right rein, leg-yielding to the left leg (the leg close to the wall) at the walk.*

especially the collection are absent in leg-yielding. This movement should be properly called a movement on two tracks, but not a lateral movement in the sense understood by the classical school. The nineteenth century German authors Seeger and Steinbrecht do not even mention leg-yielding; Seidler on the other hand discusses it at some length in his *Guidelines for the Training of the Campaign Horse* (1837). The movement is firmly established in the teachings of many schools, but it is treated separately from the other lateral movements and is considered as a loosening exercise rather than one that serves to improve collection.

If the dressage experts of the FEI call it a lateral movement, they must have good reason for doing so, which they find unnecessary to explain. However, serious students of dressage must understand the different purpose of the two kinds of movement and the reasons for controversy.

As a loosening movement, leg-yielding has been practiced for a long time and has been found to serve its purpose quickly while demanding little skill on the part of the rider or the horse. And so, why do some experts continue to object to it? Probably because the opponents of leg-yielding have mostly had in mind a faulty execution of the movement. If this is the case, their objection need not be considered. If that is the case, the same objection can be made to all the lateral movements—in the wrong hands, the best medicines are dangerous!

If the purpose and aims of a movement are not clearly recognized and if it is wrongly performed because of ignorance or incapability, it will always do more harm than good. Furthermore, to force an unprepared horse to perform a certain movement willy-nilly is courting trouble. There are so-called dressage specialists who will force a good-natured but completely uneducated horse to move sideways, and will use running reins to achieve a correct outline since they have neither the patience nor the skill to produce this by honest, direct aids.

Any horse, however uneducated, can be compelled to progress forwards and sideways by placing his head to the wall, holding his nose in and ruthlessly attacking him with the leg. It may be true that it is possible to inculcate all sorts of lessons into the mind of a horse in a short space of time by using such means of coercion, but obedience will have been secured at the expense of trust and lack of constraint.

There are unmistakable signs that reveal to a knowledgeable horseman that the animal has been trained by unseemly methods. Even with the help of a person on the ground, the horse will not stand still while being mounted and will move off with his back hollowed as soon as the rider puts his foot in the stirrup. He will not go forward on a loose rein, since he has never been allowed to "chew the bit from the hand." All the movements which the horse has learned are performed with obvious effort. He loses all presence as soon as the running-reins are taken off. This so-called advanced horse cannot trot with a correct outline even along the wall of the arena unless his nose is inflexibly held in.

Every rider ought to know that no lateral movement should be taught before the horse drives himself properly to the bit on one track.

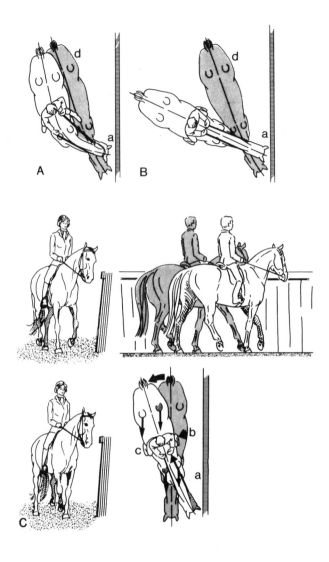

Figure 11: *Leg-yielding to the left. Incorrect:* **A** = *Excessive turning of the neck causing the outside shoulder to turn out; rider sitting crookedly.* **B** = *Insufficient forward movements, excessive lateral movement.* **C** = *Correct execution of the movement.*

The rider ought also to know what result he hopes to achieve by practicing the controversial leg-yielding exercise.

Leg-yielding must improve submission to the inside leg and hand and put the horse increasingly on the outside aids. Nobody can deny the necessity of this result. It is a loosening exercise: the horse cannot stiffen his inside hind when it is made to cross in front of the outside one and engage under the body mass; as a result, leg-yielding promotes the flexibility and elasticity of the hindquarters. Obedience to the forward and sideways-impelling leg leads to a loosening of the thoracic muscles of the same side, while the flexion of the head in the same direction loosens up the muscles of the poll.

The exercise will have achieved its principal purpose when the horse executes it as fluently to one side as to the other while maintaining a relaxed head and neck carriage and flexion of the poll, displaces himself regularly along the intended track and to either hand, and can easily be made to perform, for example, the exercise known as "enlarging and reducing the square."

Regarding correct execution of the movement, flexion of the head at the poll has to be to the same side as the sideways driving leg. The important purpose of this flexion is the relaxation of the muscles in this region to make room for the ramus of the mandible and to consequently obtain a softer tension on the inside rein and an active chewing of the bit.

The inside leg must act in the region of the girth, in the position which results quite naturally from sitting to the inside as when riding on a circle. Many riders use the inside leg too far back, especially when the horse does not yield willingly, in the mistaken belief that the further back the lower leg, the more effective it is. On the contrary, it is when the leg acts at the girth (front vertical line of boot at the edge of the girth), that the leg produces the optimum impulsive effect. It may, however, have to be supported by whip or spur in order to allow the leg to find its right place and to enable light pressures to produce the desired effect, the horse relaxing the muscles of this area.

If the horse refuses to yield to the leg, or to displace himself on two tracks and move the inside hind across the path of the outside hind, one must conclude that he is not ready for this particular lesson. The rider should return to the practice of circles, loops and voltes on a single track, which all accustom the inside leg to carry a greater share of the weight. One should also return to the lessons of the turn on the forehand, a movement closely associated with leg-yielding; it is very likely that a horse that will not yield to the leg does not execute the turn on the forehand correctly either.

As a preparation for true dressage, the turn on the forehand has limited value since as the greater proportion of weight has to be on the forehand, whereas the first aim of dressage training is to teach the horse to move in horizontal equilibrium with the ultimate aim being to get the hindquarters to support the greater proportion of the total mass. Turns

Figure 12: *Turn on the forehand.* **a** = *Track;* **b** = *Second track;* **c** = *Action of the inside leg;* **d** = *Restraining action of the outside leg;* **e** = *Return to the track.*

on the forehand should not, therefore, continue to be practiced once the horse executes them correctly without hesitation. Nevertheless, the turn on the forehand is a necessary lesson at the beginning of training as it is an easy way of acquainting the horse with the predominant effect of the rider's inside leg.

Let's now consider the essential elements of the turn on the forehand. First, one proceeds along the long side on the track and comes to a halt (Figure 12).

The horse's head must be turned towards the inside leg of the rider, which must not act before the head position is established. There is plenty of time to establish the flexion of the head since the exercise is started from the halt, but the rider must not forget to lengthen the outside rein to the same extent as he shortens the inside one. The tension of the inside rein should not be increased if the horse resists, but instead be passively maintained until the horse complies. The flexion must then be tactfully limited by the outside hand. The inside rein acts rather like a side-rein, neither giving nor pulling. As soon as the horse relaxes the tension on the inside rein and starts chewing the bit, pressures of the rider's inside leg ask for the displacement of the hindquarters, step by step. The forehand remains practically on the same spot and the inside hind must step in front and across the outside one. The horse can never be allowed to cross the inside hind behind the outside one.

If the horse disregards the normal pressure of the inside leg, the rider, instead of using more and useless strength or thumping with his boot, should reinforce his leg aid with either a light or a firm touch of the whip. Neither strenuous pressure of leg nor use of the spur are as effective in obtaining prompt obedience to the leg than the immediate resort to the whip whenever the horse chooses to "turn a deaf ear" to the moderate pressure of the lower leg.

Considerate use of the whip reveals a rider's experience and tact. A barely perceptible touch may be all that is required in the case of a sensitive horse, but quite a sharp smack may be required to persuade a particularly dull one. It is, however, unwise at this early stage of the horse's education to resort to a painful blow that could easily destroy the animal's trust in the rider. The horse must respect the whip but not to fear it. A horse that reacts by panic to the sight of a whip when worked on the lunge or being ridden has probably had to suffer at some time unreasonably harsh application of this indispensable persuader.

While the outside hand limits the flexion of the head and neck, the outside leg, acting behind the girth, limits at each step the displacement of the outside hind. If it were too big a sideways step, it would be difficult if not impossible for the inside hind to step across the outside hind again. To ensure that the horse does not come off the aids but maintains a faultless carriage during the execution of the movement, the rider must urge him forward to the bit by using seat (bracing the small of the back) and both legs. In fact, this supposedly elementary exercise requires a very precise and skillful combination of all the aids; the horse must be seen to step smoothly and regularly around his forehand with his hind legs at a rhythm rather similar to that of the medium trot.

Exactly the same aids as for the turn on the forehand apply to leg-yielding. The inside leg commands the forward-sideways movement and the outside leg, behind the girth, must be ready to limit the sideways displacement as soon as the horse has yielded to the action of the inside leg. Many riders neglect to use the outside leg with the result that the hindquarters turn out or the outside hind is displaced sideways to such an extent that the subsequent crossing in front of it by the inside is impossible. The gait loses its purity and degenerates into an ugly lateral shambling.

If leg-yielding is practiced in such a manner that the horse has to move almost at a right angle to the wall, an audible knocking of bone against bone usually occurs as well. It is not surprising that purist adherents to classical methods object so strongly to this exercise if that is how they believe that it is usually executed! Nevertheless, always provided that the horse is adequately educated and remains constantly between the aids of both hands and both legs, the movement is a fluent, undemanding forward-lateral one—without collection — that loosens the horse effectively from head to tail. A calm horse animated by impulsion will perform leg-yielding with consummate ease and apparently even with enjoyment.

Although the purpose of the exercise is not really to produce flexion of head and neck (it can be executed correctly without any degree of flexion), in fact, owing to the position of the rider's legs which is the same as on circles and loops, a very slight degree of general bend is usual. This is merely a by-product of the lesson and a very welcome one indeed.

There are ways other than the one described above of executing the movement and of utilizing the lesson. The horse can be asked to displace himself from the inside to the outside track and vice versa, to enlarge or diminish the square, or to enlarge the circle on the open side.

Enlarging the volte by getting the horse to yield to the inside leg is an exercise rarely practiced nowadays, but it still remains as a useful corrective one in the case of a horse that persistently refuses to engage his inside hind. Briefly, it can be described as a turn on the forehand in forward movement on a circle of six to ten meters diameter; its dimension must allow the horse to continue to move at a regular walk or trot.

Also for the same purpose of getting young horses to engage their inside hind, one can begin the exercise by making them yield to the inside leg (i.e. the inside leg in relation to the arena). The wall acts as a barrier that prevents rushing and helps in maintaining direction. One should, however, beware of driving the horse's head against the wall and making him measure the length of the wall with his nose! To avoid this faulty performance of the exercise, it is advisable to cut the corner a little and, at that point, to produce a slight degree of flexion and start the leg-yielding indication just before the horse's forefeet reach the next side. Thus the position is already obtained as one gets on the track.

A gross error consists in teaching leg-yielding by suddenly just turning the head of the horse towards the wall while the animal is proceeding straight along the track and then making him yield to the outside leg, driving his hindquarters on an inside track. This teaches the horse to disengage the hindquarters, and the result of this misguided lesson will be discovered at a later stage when a lateral movement must be performed on the centerline (as is frequently required nowadays in tests). The horse will develop the disagreeable habit of preceding the forehand with the hindquarters.

It is advisable, therefore, to use the above form of leg-yielding (forehand to the wall) only for as long as may be necessary to get the horse to understand that he is supposed to move sideways as well as forward and thereafter to make him move forward and sideways from the outside track to the inside one. This obviates many of the disadvantages of the exercise and is a useful preparation for the shoulder-in.

Leg-yielding on the open side of a circle is another way of obtaining the desired result. The movement is started like a half-volte onto the inside track, with the horse being made to cross behind after the point of leaving the wall. But it is not easy to maintain an even circle and this exercise is more demanding for the horse since it requires more extensive crossing over of the inside hind.

Enlarging or decreasing the turning of the corner is, as has already been said, a useful corrective measure that helps to oblige a horse with a lazy hind leg to engage it effectively

Although it is rarely used, one of the easiest methods of teaching the lesson to both horse and rider is to get them to turn onto the centerline and then to proceed forwards and sideways towards the

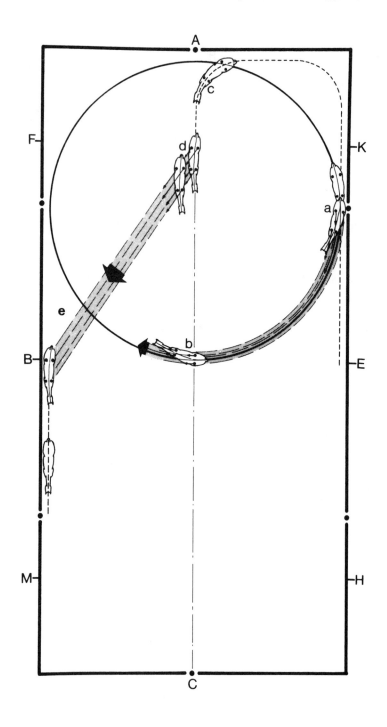

Figure 13: **a, b** = *Leg-yielding on the circle.* **c, d, e** = *Leg-yielding from the centerline towards the middle of the long side.*

middle of the opposite long side of the arena while maintaining the flexion required in the turn.

There are, therefore, several forms of varying degrees of difficulty of practicing this exercise. An experienced horseman will choose the one most appropriate to circumstances, but will always start with the least demanding one.

Riders frequently ask at what stage of a horse's education they should start teaching yielding to the leg. This cannot be precisely stated, but is certainly not before the horse can maintain a fluent, regular working trot on straight lines or on large circles in a correct outline and chewing the bit. So much depends on the aptitudes of rider and horse. Tumultuous sideways movement by a tense horse is of no beneficial use at all and can even lead to injury to his limbs. Forcing the horse to move sideways in the hope of correcting gross crookedness before he has been taught to obey the outside aids by work on the circle is a grave error. This cannot be stressed too strongly. Leg-yielding can certainly enhance the loosening and the flexion obtained by work on the circle on a single track, but it is also a fact that no other exercise, with the exception of the flying change (which will be discussed), is more likely to produce disastrous results than leg-yielding when it is prematurely introduced and ineptly executed.

When a young horse endowed with ideal conformation and temperament for dressage is trained from the beginning of his education by a knowledgeable and capable horseman, the lesson is certainly not essential. In the course of his training the shoulder-in, from which all other lateral movements evolve, the measure of collection and the bend required at each stage will be produced. There are, however, many horses with less than ideal aptitudes and many that have been badly trained and badly ridden for months or years, and are either stiff, crooked, wrongly bent, resistant to the leg, constrained or deficient in all those respects. They may even stubbornly refuse to turn on the forehand to both sides. Fortunate indeed is the rider who never has to cope with any of those difficulties but he is also rare! Professional trainers and riders of modest financial means cannot be too choosey. In their case, leg-yielding is a proven loosening exercise that can enable them to achieve within a reasonably short period of time at least modest improvement in the manner of going of their mount. It can be argued that the same result can be obtained by strictly classical methods, provided one has endless patience and is resigned to the long and tedious work required. Few riders, however, have either the time or the necessary knowledge to undertake such a demanding task. Yet training capable but difficult horses is interesting work that is well rewarded by their eventual accomplishment. They may never take their rider to the top in competition and, purely from this point of view, time spent on them may well be wasted. But a rider who has never had to overcome the problems posed by difficult horses will never become a completely proficient horseman. It cannot be denied that the lesson in leg-yielding is a convenient and effective corrective method that can shorten the preparation for collecting work. The aim of leg-yielding is limited but clear and attainment of this aim is easy to assess. It should form part of the repertoire of every rider in any riding disciplines. We should neither condemn the exercise out of hand, nor overestimate its value. It is a necessary stage in the education of most horses which can only be skipped if one has the good luck to discover an exceptional horse that does not need to be taught this lesson.

Chapter 6

The Half-Pirouette in Walk

The turn on the haunches and the walk pirouette are not just about turning on the spot; specifically, they are very collected movements. Anybody who in the course of a career in horsemanship will have to ride, teach or judge hundreds of these turns must have a clear conception of their correct execution, for the opportunity to see a turn on the haunches or a half-pirouette at the walk conforming to the rules of classical dressage is rarely granted. There are too many riders who do not seem to understand the purpose of the movement.

It ought to be considered mainly as a means of progressively furthering the education of the dressage horse. It is not intended to just teach the horse to turn about rapidly and safely in a restricted space, but to stimulate the activity of the hind limbs when they carry the greater proportion of the combined weight of horse and rider. It is a movement designed to improve collection and flexion of the haunches. It is also meant to heighten the sensitivity of the horse to the forward and lateral driving actions of the legs, and to the restraining actions of the hands and as such is an important lesson in submission.

We should note the difference between a turn *about* the haunches and a turn *on* the haunches. The first term merely indicates a pivoting of the mass about its center of movement, but does not imply a rearward shifting of the weight. A turn *on* the haunches, on the other hand, definitely requires that the turn be executed around the point of support constituted by the inside hind foot.

The lesson is important also from the point of view of the rider's education. It makes greater demands than most movements on his ability to use all the aids (especially those of outside leg and hand), with feeling and in precise timing. It reveals clearly to the judge the quality of the rider as well as the degree of suppleness and impulsion of the horse and his state of readiness for collected work, or in other words, the horse's degree of tractability.

In contrast with the turn on the haunches which starts and ends with a square halt, the walk pirouette is a turn on the haunches proceeding uninterruptedly from the collected walk and immediately succeeded by a return to forward movement. It is always done from the walk. A transition to the walk has therefore to be executed whenever a walk pirouette is indicated after a movement at trot or canter; the pirouette is started as soon as the walk is established, and the forward movement at the previous gait is resumed immediately on completion of the pirouette. This is certainly feasible, but it demands considerable agility and submission on the part of the horse.

Since it is the walk pirouette that is usually required in modern tests, it is on this movement that we will concentrate our attention. We will start by describing a perfect execution of this elegant and useful exercise—this will make the flaws all the more obvious. Since the purpose of the movement is to improve collection, one must presume that a sufficient state of collection will already have been established before the commencement of the turn. This is most easily maintained in the walk.

Before the beginning of the turn the horse must be evenly bent from head to tail in the direction of the movement. This is a rule that applies, of course, to all changes of direction (except the turn on the forehand, in which the flexion of the head alone suffices), because it is overall bend that effectively puts both sides of the horse under the control of the rider. The walk pirouette is a turn in travers position, with the hindquarters describing a shorter path than the forehand. The steps behind must therefore be shortened, which explains the necessity for collection, i.e. the lightening of the forehand by transfer of weight to the hindquarters. The rider must decide in how many steps of the walk he intends to complete the turn. He should not allow circumstances or the horse to dictate matters, but nor should the number of steps be officially prescribed; this would make the test much too demanding for the majority of horse and riders.

After a half halt the rider gives the aids for the turn and then continues to use his seat as well as his legs to activate alternately both hind limbs and to continually to drive the horse to the bit and become "rounder," thus maintaining or even increasing the degree of collection in which the turn was commenced.

A correct pirouette can be obtained only if the hind feet can be caused to make a sufficient number of short, distinct steps. Towards this purpose, it is essential for the rider to create impulsion not just with his legs but also with his firmly braced lower back; this bracing enables the hands to oppose the forward movement without actively pulling. The outside hand supports the inside leg in producing the displacement of the forehand on the larger circle; the inside hand preserves the bend and the softness of contact. Seat and legs have the dominant role and if the hands are seen to be unduly active, as is so often the case, it reveals that the rider is unable to use his lower aids effectively. He must, of course, sit to the inside to oblige the inside hind to carry the greater share of the weight and flex all its joints, but also because his inside leg

54

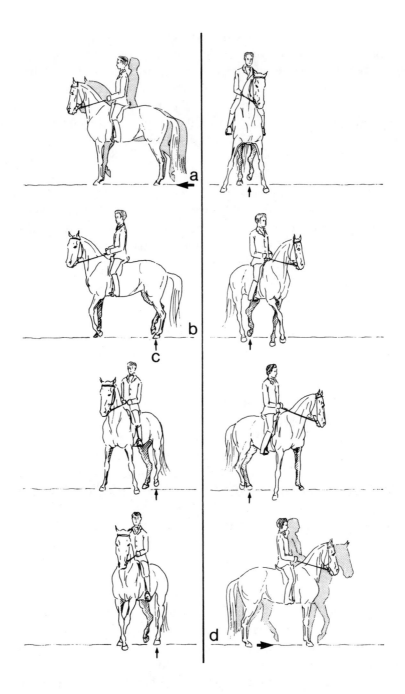

Figure 14: *Turn on the haunches.* **a** = *Transition to complete halt;* **b** = *Preparation of the turn;* **c** = *Activity of the inside hind;* **d** = *End of the turn: halt; proceed forwards.*

must be used to greater effect to ensure that the loaded inside hind foot steps regularly on a very small half circle.

It is impossible to produce collection and the essential activity of the horse's hind feet with either tapping or squeezing legs. The seemingly prevalent belief that cadenced steps are obtained by mighty gripping with the calves is a very serious error, against which riders cannot be too strongly warned. Muscular force is entirely useless in feeling and preventing the immobility of one hind foot or a backward step. It also dulls the horse's reactions and does not permit the fine variations of leg pressures that the dressage horse must be taught to understand and respond to.

Whenever a movement is executed within very short confines, be it a half-pirouette at the walk, a canter-pirouette or piaffe, the activity of the hindquarters can be maintained only by agility in the use of the legs supported, if necessary, by enlivening touches in rapid succession with the spurs. This nimbleness is possible only if the legs always remain in light and sensitive contact with the horse's sides.

Using all one's strength to wrest a step out of a horse is as pointless as trying to squeeze a stone to draw from it a few drops of water. Nevertheless, one often sees riders attempting to execute the half-pirouette who give the impression that superhuman force is needed to stir their horse out of his lethargy.

Although it is not the only criterion by which to judge the half-pirouette or the canter-pirouette, the number of the steps executed in the turn does give a good indication of its quality. It is certainly feasible to execute the turn in three or four big steps, but since there is then no collection, the movement cannot be considered as a correct half-pirouette. Turning the forehand around totally motionless hind feet does not rate as a half-pirouette either. At least six regular steps must be seen; eight is about average; ten is pretty good (the number must, of course, be an even one) and twelve is unnecessarily difficult. In the latter case, in order to tread with his hind feet on a very small circle and to be able to obey the indications of the rider's legs, the horse would have to be performing piaffe!

Half-pirouettes in piaffe have not yet been required in any test. However, Article 412, section 2 of the FEI *Rules for Dressage* definitely states: "Pirouettes (half-pirouettes) are normally performed at the collected walk or canter but they can be executed at the piaffe." Half-pirouette in the piaffe may be required in years to come; who knows what the future holds in store for us? There would certainly be some advantages in executing pirouettes in piaffe, advantages which I will mention but briefly since a long discussion would exceed the scope of this work.   Nevertheless, some dressage specialists might be disappointed if nothing was said on the subject.   Others will surely forgive me for this digression.

First, it is evident that the bend required for the half-pirouette—a bend that necessitates the use of the guarding outside leg—compels the horse to compact his body more on the side of the turn. This enables the rider to activate more easily the lazy hind limb of the stiff side of the horse. The turn in piaffe obliges the horse to step energetically behind. More weight is transferred to the hindquarters and their joints must flex more, thus lightening the forehand which consequently becomes easier to displace on the larger circle. Those results are not easy to obtain at the walk.

The pseudo-piaffe with disengaged hocks in which the horse maintains his weight on the forehand is quite impossible in the half-pirouette. I will have more to say in a subsequent chapter on the subject of turns in piaffe or passage, but while on the subject of the half-

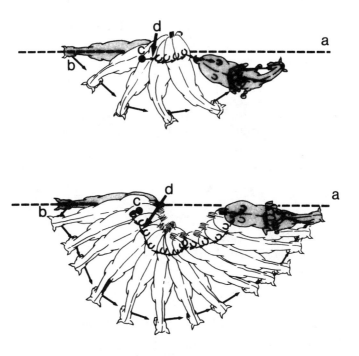

Figure 15: *Faulty turn on the haunches. Above:* **a** = *Track;* **b** = *Excessive bending of neck of a horse being dragged round by the hands;* **c** *and* **d** = *Inside hind stepping backwards.   Below:* **a** = *Track;* **b** = *Tilting of the horse's head;* **c** = *Irregular insufficiently collected half-circle with lateral deviation of the croup;* **d** = *Inside hind evades it supporting duty.*

pirouette, let me say that one should always think more about the maintenance of the piaffe than about the exact execution of the turn. The same applies to the canter pirouette. The maintenance of the gait is what matters most.

In reality I have not digressed much from the subject of the half-pirouette because all the elements of the piaffe, in an attenuated form, are present in a truly classical half-pirouette at the walk. It is significant that formerly in the Grand Prix test the first transition to passage had to be executed out of the half-pirouette.

Riders, teachers, trainers or judges will no doubt admit that a perfectly correct walk pirouette is a rare sight nowadays. The reason for this appears to be that the importance of the movement as a means of furthering the education of horse and rider and improving collection is generally underestimated. But besides neglecting to work the movement, it does seem that many riders have a wrong conception of what constitutes a classical half-pirouette. In most instances it is ridden as if the major consideration was the about-turn, whereas it really should be a means of setting the horse on his haunches in the shortest possible time as a thorough preparation for collected work. There is little excuse for not working towards this end because the half-pirouette can be taught practically anywhere: in the smallest ring, in crowded riding halls (but then preferably not on the outside track), or on any kind of ground.

The fact that the educational value of the exercise is generally overlooked is obvious when one observes riders putting their horses through their paces before a test. In the lower levels it is all trot, canter, trot, canter and, after an interval of walk on a loose rein to allow horse and rider to recuperate, again trot, canter, trot, canter. At medium levels and above there is more variety and we can see half pass, extended gaits, flying changes and at a higher level still, piaffe, passage and canter-pirouette, but only rarely a halt and only rarely any attention to self-carriage and cadence. One sees even more rarely any work at the walk, and the half-pirouette, rein back and *Schaukel* are very much neglected. Yet it is in the half-pirouette and the *Schaukel* that a horse's crookedness is most easily noticed. One suspects that quite a number of riders fail to appreciate the real reason for the annoying inclusion in tests of these deceptively simple movements, for which there are not many marks to be gained in any case even provided that they are executed somehow at the prescribed place.

Let us now consider the most serious flaws of the half-pirouette. And to start with it must be understood that the German word for the half-pirouette, *Kurzkehr*, meaning "sharp about-turn" does not signify a quick turn. If the horse or the rider throws the forehand round rapidly, the hind feet cannot possibly make a sufficient number of steps. On the other hand, a slow, hesitant turn with pauses between the steps is equally faulty; it demonstrates either the ineffectiveness of the rider or the resistance of the horse. Generally, a slow turn with rather blurred though regular hind steps is less severely judged than a rushed and irregular turn. In the scale of marks, regularity of the steps comes a close second in importance to purity of the walk. However, to deserve earning a good mark for the half-pirouette, the horse should turn in the sequence of the walk with well engaged hocks and in *lively* hind steps.

Frequently, horses will remain "stuck" on the rider's outside leg and will turn abruptly by declining to obey the rider's inside leg. During schooling the best way to correct the fault is to execute the turn in isolated steps. By this I mean that the rider does not permit another step before he has the previous one under control. In this case it is advisable to use the turn on the haunches, from the halt to the halt, rather than the half-pirouette. It has the effect of curbing the impatience of the horse and obliging the rider to be more precise in the use of his aids.

The next more prevalent fault is the consequence of thinking more about turning than about collection. In this case the rider neglects to use his legs and pulls the forehand into the turn with the inside rein, thereby bending only the head and neck of the horse. The horse immediately turns out his hindquarters and executes a sort of turn about the center instead of a turn on the haunches. Alternately, the hind feet remain rooted to the ground while the forehand is hauled around (one can sometimes distinctly hear the clicking of hind joints). One corrects this fault by having the horse work diligently on two tracks; a helpful exercise is a half-pass at the walk towards the center of the arena ending in a half-volte on two tracks wherein the hind feet step on a half-circle of approximately 50 cm radius. The half-pass will have produced the required bend which is maintained in the half-volte; the radius of the half-circle can be gradually decreased as the horse's agility improves.

Since the principles applying to the half-pirouette at the walk and the canter-pirouette are the same, the latter should be ridden and corrected in much the same manner as the former.

However, it is interesting to note that when a horse is insufficiently collected in a canter pirouette, many judges will remark "blurred steps," "lack of expression," "insufficient elevation," "hocks disengaged," etc., but very few judges will mark down a walk pirouette for insufficient collection. For example, here is a typical comment on a half-pirouette in which the horse was blatantly on the forehand, let alone not sufficiently collected: "distinct and regular steps, almost on the spot, impulsion good, etc." The judges were evidently just counting the steps behind, failing to notice and take into consideration the defective outline, the lack of animation, the elevated croup and lowered head and neck.

Another frequent defect is insufficient or absent uniform bend making a correct pirouette totally impossible. It is the bend which enables the rider to make the horse engage his hocks; the rider cannot prevent a trailing of the hind limbs if the horse resists the combined aids, nor can he elicit the regular, lively steps that ensure a fluent turn. A stiffened inside hind then easily finds ways and means of avoiding the inconvenience of having to carry the major part of the weight, and the turning out of the outside hind cannot be prevented. A horse that will not bend correctly will also not respond willingly, if at all, to the aids and cannot be taught to perform any lesson fluently. Fluency depends entirely on the development of reflex obedience to finely graduated leg effects. Therefore, before starting to teach such difficult movements as the half-pirouette or the canter pirouette, it is essential to develop the suppleness of the horse gradually by work in forward movement on circles, voltes and serpentines and correct work on two tracks along the wall. Eventually the half-pirouette can be executed immediately after one or more voltes at a determined spot which will ensure that the about-turn is started with the horse already properly bent in the direction of the turn.

Should a horse absolutely refuse to turn (a not infrequent occurrence when starting to teach the half-pirouette), one should remember the ancient prescription to start the movement by making the horse step forward one step or driving him forwards and sideways in a half-pass before asking for the turn. To prevent the backward step that many horses will understandably attempt to make, every step of the half-pirouette should be ridden with a tendency to move forward.

An excellent method of teaching the half-pirouette is as follows:

One rides the horse at an active collected walk in a slight travers position on a square volte each side of which measures 8 m. Having to tread on the shorter inside track especially in the corner, the hindquarters must shorten their steps and support an increased share of the weight, thus enhancing collection. If the walk remains lively, in proper sequence of four footfalls, the corner can be turned as a quarter of a pirouette. Once this exercise is completely mastered, the half-pirouette, or even a three-quarter or a complete pirouette can eventually be achieved, although it is always preferable to spend more time on the preparation of the movement than on its actual execution. Horses that

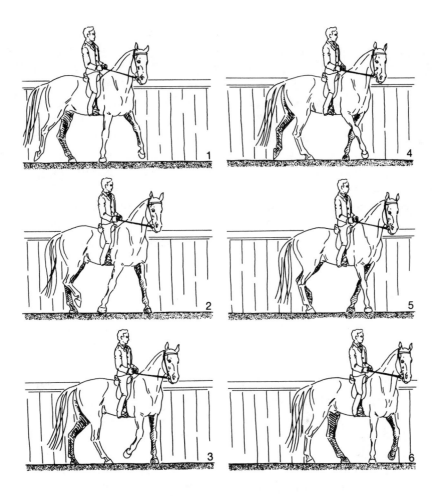

Figure 16 : *Shoulder-in at the walk along the wall*

have mastered the exercise described above have never been known to have any difficulty in executing the half-pirouette.

Having considered mainly the shortcomings in the education of the horse which are revealed by the half-pirouette, let us now examine the rider. It must be noted that the half-pirouette more than any other dressage movement requires absolutely perfect coordination of the aids. Not even the most accomplished of dressage horses will ever execute a half-pirouette of his own accord! The way he rides a half-pirouette shows more clearly than the collected trot or the canter whether a rider is ready to compete in elementary tests. Keen, properly schooled horses can perform these latter movements without much assistance from the rider. The medium and extended trot, circles and voltes in a relative degree of collection are intended to demonstrate the gaits and tractability of horse but they do not always prove the superior competence of the rider. However, dressage tests ought not be just demonstrations of the combined arts of nature, breeder and trainer; they should also reveal the ability of the rider. This is not evidenced so much by spectacular extensions as by the fluency of the correct halts and the correctness of the rein back and the half-pirouette—yet these are movements which many riders do not seem to consider particularly significant.

The counter-canter, the medium trot, and the flying changes are movements that many horses execute of their own accord when at liberty; not so the regular half-pirouette. It is against the horse's instinct to change direction in such a strenuous manner, which is one reason why in the past as much as nowadays "practical riders" have often condemned "school riding," seeing it as perversion of natural movement. According to them: "The art of dressage consists in making the horse move in the most uneconomical manner possible, on as restricted a space as possible over the longest possible period of time!"

After limited experience of watching dressage tests, it is not difficult to notice gross faults in the execution of the half-pirouette. A not-so-obvious fault often committed by relatively inexperienced riders of well-trained horses is the "side-slip." The rider uses the outside aids of rein, leg and whip to make the horse turn and neglects to use the inside aids. The inside hind is thus enabled to evade its duty by stepping sideways; consequently too many steps are needed to complete the turn and the half-pirouette ends well beyond the spot where it was started (Figure 15). How can the fault be corrected? By shoulder-in at the walk before and after the turn which is executed on the centerline or on some other line parallel to the wall. This allows one to practice the turn a number of times in the same direction until the execution is satisfactory, which is of course impossible if the turn is performed on the track against the wall.

It would take too long to enumerate all the faults riders can commit in the execution of the movement and to describe the means of correction. However, there is no getting away from the fact that it is only by practicing the half-pirouette or the turn on the haunches sufficiently frequently that one learns to do it correctly. It does not make one dizzy. A rider who does not know how to bend a horse and how to collect him, who has not trained himself conscientiously until he has mastered completely the necessary subtle coordination of aids, will perpetually remain incapable of performing a correct turn of this kind.

The movement is a difficult one for the horse as well as the rider and one cannot hope for perfection every time. Moreover, the half-pirouette prescribed in elementary tests cannot be expected to be executed on as small a circle as in a Grand Prix. But it is a sure indication of insufficient education of one or the other if a supposedly advanced horse or rider consistently fails to produce a perfect half-pirouette, and something urgently needs to be done to make good the shortcomings of either horse or rider. Although it may not impress the gallery as much as other movements, the half-pirouette is the most revealing test of proficiency of the rider and shows whether he has done his home work painstakingly or shirked the difficult bits. This is probably why at dressage events one so rarely sees the movement being practiced before the test. On the other hand, a correctly executed half-pirouette in the test ought to be more generously rated and remarked upon by the judges than it usually is. They should not be so sparing of their compliments.

Specifically for the purpose of improving collection, the movement should be included in all the work at the collected walk that comes in between the work at the trot and the work at the canter. A lesson in the collected walk is inconceivable without the inclusion of halt, rein backs and half-pirouettes, and it is essential to be able to check on the proper sequence of the steps of the walk by making use of mirrors in the riding hall. In the past the favored place for the execution of those lessons was opposite a mirror on the long side of the arena; nowadays this place is usually deserted.

Still, there is a way of verifying the correct execution of the half-pirouette if one cannot use a mirror. It consists in approaching the spot for the half-pirouette at a collected trot and proceeding at the trot immediately after completion of the turn. The trot after the half-pirouette should be slower, more cadenced, more lively than before the turn. If not, if the horse just runs along in a flat, hurried "dogtrot" after the turn, the latter cannot have been executed correctly and has failed its real purpose, the enhancement of collection.

Chapter 7

Shoulder-In and
Counter Shoulder-In

The horse ridden in straight position is committed to a straight line; the correctly bent horse is committed to a curved line. Nevertheless, a bent horse can proceed along a straight line provided one allows him to cross his outside hind or outside fore in front of the respective inside ones.

This simple but inspired discovery is the basis of all the so-called lateral movements. However, it must be emphasized that the crossing of limbs is not the purpose of the exercises but, rather, the result of the bending.

The lateral movements serve more than one purpose and are so essential in the education of the dressage horse that, beyond a certain stage, he must do them every day, like piano performers do the scales and ballet dancers work at the bar to improve their agility.

The primary purpose of the lateral movements is to develop gradually, and equally to both sides, the normally limited lateral suppleness of the horse's trunk. But they have other important purposes as well. They inhibit the purely forward-driving effect of the movements of the hind limbs, obliging the hind limbs to function as flexible props that allow the forehand to be relieved of some of the weight. This is particularly useful in the case of very forward-going horses that are difficult to control and collect on a single track. Additionally, lateral movements improve the agility and responsiveness to the aids of horses fairly advanced in their education, therefore improving their submissiveness also. Moreover the lateral movements, when correctly executed, enhance the flexion of the haunches, the elasticity and the propelling power of the hind limbs with the result that the steps in the extended gaits gain in scope and expression.

Besides these advantages of lateral movements in general, each individual movement has a special purpose which will be considered later. Taken altogether, they provide the rider with a variety of means of improving a horse's tractability.

It must, however, be emphasized that two track movements can only serve those purposes on the condition that they are impeccably executed. When wrongly executed, they have very serious drawbacks and in equitational matters, as in all others, we ought to remember that too much of a good thing can be as harmful as too little. It is, of course, impossible to prescribe a dosage to suit all cases. The art of horsemanship is not like the art of cookery in which the ingredients of a recipe have to be measured with precision.

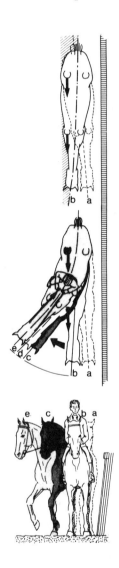

Figure 17: **a** = *Position of young and/or partly trained horse hugging the wall with his shoulder;* **b** = *Straightened position (inside shoulder in line with inside hip);* **c** = *Minimum degree of shoulder-in, approximately 30 degrees, for the first lessons; inside hind stepping in the track of outside fore;* **d** = *Medial position, approximately 35 degrees;* **e** = *Extreme position; four tracks clearly marked. Note that for the sake of clarity in the bottom sketch position* **d** *is not shown.*

It requires great experience in training and riding many different horses to be able to decide unerringly to which hand, on which line, in which sequence and for how long the various two tracks movements should be practiced in each case. Less experienced riders should always allow themselves to be guided by an expert if they want to avoid the consequences of inappropriate and bungled execution of any of the lateral movements.

This chapter concerns the shoulder-in and, to start with, we should note that it is necessary to teach even young horses at the beginning of training to move straight along the wall of the arena. This is done by riding them "in position," i.e. in a very slight degree of shoulder-in.

Nearly all young horses tend to hug the wall with hips and shoulders and, since their hips are broader than their shoulders, they move them in a rather crablike manner.

To get them to move straight one must move the shoulders to the inside a little so that the inside shoulder is in front of the inside hip and the inside fore and hind feet mark one track. The rider's outside leg, assisted by the presence of the wall, must ensure that the outside hind does not move outward, while the rider's inside leg ensures that the inside hind remains in line with the inside fore. It may not be possible to establish this position from the first days of schooling, but one should persevere. One cannot start straightening a horse too soon and it is a mistake to allow young horses to simply run along in the position which they find most convenient.

The shoulder-fore, as the position described above is known, entails a very small degree of bend and prepares the horse for the proper shoulder-in. Horses that have been trained to the shoulder-fore will show much less resistance to the shoulder-in than horses that have been allowed to move as they please.

Two track work proper may be started as soon as a horse can easily maintain the appropriate bend on circles, voltes and serpentines, and fluently reverse his bend on request. It is better to start with the shoulder-in because it makes it easier for the horse to understand the strange new requirement of his rider. Moreover, in the shoulder-in one can avail oneself of the presence of the wall; it is a very useful auxiliary aid for the teaching of all new lessons (Figure 18).

There has always been disagreement regarding the optimum angle for the shoulder-in, with some maintaining that the feet should mark four tracks on the ground, and others insisting that only three should be seen.

It all depends, of course, on the degree of suppleness of the horse.

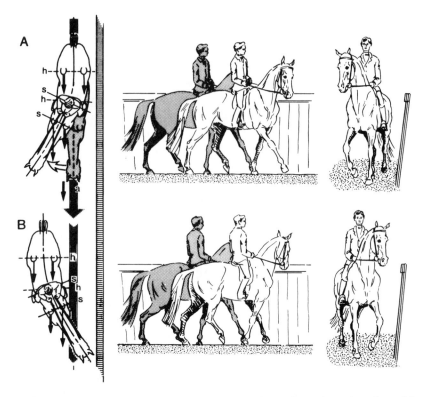

Figure 18: **A** = *Right shoulder-in at the trot (viewed from above, from the side and from the front)*; **B** = *left counter shoulder-in at the trot*; **h** = *Rider's and horse's hips*; **s** = *Rider's and horse's shoulders.*

In the minimum degree of shoulder-in, the inside hind must step in the track of the outside fore; if one observes the horse from the front or the rear, three tracks can be seen. This is a sufficient degree for the ordinary riding horse and for tests of medium difficulty. In the most advanced tests, if a horse is supple enough to execute correctly a six meter volte on one track, he should be capable of doing a shoulder-in that is really on two tracks (four hoof marks traced on the ground).

The latter form is rarely shown in modern dressage tests; there are too few riders who have the time to train a horse to attain such an extreme degree of suppleness. It is the reason why for some time now the smallest diameter of a volte has been set at six meters in international tests. It used to be six strides of 80 cm = 4 m 80, which required the utmost possible degree of bend; it would then have been logical to expect a highly proficient horse to be able to perform a shoulder-in in extreme position marking four tracks on the ground. However, the horse would have to be able to do this to both hands with equal ease.

Although he does not say so in so many words, sketches illustrating his work and his description of the movement indicate that its inventor, de La Gueriniere, intended it to be performed in its extreme form.

Therefore, in Prix St. George, a shoulder-in on the centerline executed with the maximum possible degree of bend (four tracks) is perfectly correct, but one that imprinted only three tracks would be sufficient. The former, however, should be rated higher. In any case the bend must be uniform, without a break at the withers, and without any tilting of the poll. The gait must be regular and expressive, very collected and the horse must move in self-carriage.

Nowadays in international competitions under FEI rules, two track movements have to be performed on the centerline, thus ruling out any possibility of deception; the rider is obliged to lay his cards on the table. It is conceivable that in the future at the highest level of difficulty a change of hand on the centerline will be required; the submissiveness of the horse truly would be demonstrated if he were seen to change with total fluency from one position to the opposite one.

In the course of schooling, a sensitive rider will be able to feel when the horse is ready to start learning the lateral movements. Nevertheless one can expect various resistances even from carefully prepared horses. Some will attempt to evade the difficulty of preserving their bend on straight lines by turning out their outside hind. Others will try to step backwards (a possibility denied to them to a considerable extent by the wall of the arena), or will tend to move away from the track towards the center of the arena. Even horses familiarized with forward and sideways movement by the practice of leg-yielding will experience a measure of discomfort when first asked for a shoulder-in because of the new requirement of uniform bend from head to tail. It is therefore advisable to stop the practice of leg-yielding as soon as the horse executes it without difficulty to both hands and to start teaching the shoulder-in instead so that the horse does not get into the habit of moving forward and sideways without, or with insufficient, bend.

In the first lessons it is essential to limit the displacement of the forehand to only a very small degree, as the rider's outside leg must be able to hold the hindquarters on their track and to help maintain the direction and the bend. The quality of a shoulder-in must be determined by the degree of bend of the horse, not by the degree of angle in the position. The two things must not be confused for it is essential to maintain impulsion and regularity of gait and both would suffer if the position were exaggerated in a degree of angle that was too severe.

"Quarters-out" instead of shoulder-in is the worst of all faults except for irregularity of gait. For this reason it is essential that the rider use a correct "bending seat," with his weight to the inside, his inside leg at the girth where it can best exert the forward and sideways driving influence, and his outside leg somewhat further back to compel the hindquarters to remain on their assigned track.

The movement is started after the corner of the arena has been passed with the horse properly bent in the turn. With both reins (the inside one predominant), the shoulders are brought onto the inside track, and then the rider's inside leg and outside rein prescribe the direction. Additionally, the outside rein, though allowing the stretching of the horse's outside neck muscles, must prevent more bend in of the neck than in the rib cage which would cause the horse to load his outside shoulder. The inside hand, assisted by the outside leg, maintains the softness of the contact. The reins must not pull the horse sideways and their line of action must therefore be in the direction of the rider's chest.

The rider's shoulders should be parallel to the horse's shoulders.

Contrary to the general rule, in the shoulder-in the rider must not keep his sight on a line passing between the horse's ears, but must instead keep it on the line of the track that the horse has to follow; otherwise he cannot possible accurately judge from his position in the saddle whether the horse is moving exactly on the prescribed track.

The shoulder-in seat is sometimes called the turning seat because it necessitates a horizontal rotation of the various segments of the rider's body about a vertical axis. The rider's head and neck are turned in the direction of the track, his chest and shoulders must be turned somewhat inward, parallel to the horse's shoulders, and his outside hip must be held back to correspond with the position of his outside leg. In fact, the rider's position thus conforms to the horse's position.

The seat just described must not be strained; the rider should be able to maintain it with ease. It is therefore not advisable to teach riders to perform lateral movements before they are able to maintain a correct seat easily in all movements on one track.

A faulty seat is frequently the cause of incorrect performance by the horse of the lateral movements. A rider who is not yet able to sit upright easily lacks the suppleness which allows him to achieve the rotation of the various segments of his upper body and will be unable to control the hindquarters of the horse with his outside leg. He will be thrown forward by the horse who will then be able to turn out his hindquarters. The rider may draw his inside leg back in the mistaken belief that the more it is drawn back, the greater its effect, and consequently will sit crookedly. Also, if he cannot turn his chest and shoulders without turning his hips the same way, his reins will have the wrong effect. Those faults are all very common.

It should be evident that the rider must sit to the inside when the horse is moving in shoulder-in since the greater flexion of the horse's inside haunch causes a lowering of his inside hip. However, when teaching the movement it may sometimes be necessary to deliberately sit more heavily to the outside; this can help the horse to understand more easily in which direction he must move.

The preparation of the movement is of greatest importance. If the horse starts a lateral movement in a wrong position, enormous skill is required to correct it during the execution of the movement. It is generally better to bring the horse back to a straight position and then turn the two corners of the short side with particular attention to correct bend, and to engagement and activity of the inside hind. After the second corner, instead of abruptly pulling the shoulders onto the inside track, one brings them in gradually and smoothly. The inside leg must not start driving laterally before the point where the movement has to start. If it acts prematurely, the horse will be driven straight along the wall and the rider will find himself unable to place the shoulders sufficiently on the inside track. Regarding control of the degree of angle in shoulder-in, here is a useful tip: in a 20 x 60 m arena, if one directs the forehand at the beginning of the shoulder-in towards a point situated halfway along the opposite wall, one obtains an angle of approximately 40 degrees. By directing the forehand towards the point on the opposite wall where one would start the shoulder-in, the angle would be approximately 35 degrees. If one aims the forehand towards the corner of the arena, the angle would be about 30 degrees, and sufficient in the early stages of teaching the movement.

Once the horse can execute this mild form of shoulder-in with a sufficient degree of fluency, the lesson should be confirmed by the practice of the "counter shoulder-in." The particular advantage of this exercise is that it allows the rider to use his outside leg with greater effect, since the presence of the wall towards which the horse is turned obviates his tendency to run away from this leg.

It is much easier to obtain overall bend by means of this exercise than by means of the usual shoulder-in. Nevertheless, one must carefully guard against any tendency the horse might show to move away from the wall. This can be prevented by maintaining constantly the same degree of position in relation to the wall of the arena; the forehand can then be correctly guided (Figure 19).

As soon as the horse can execute the shoulder-in and the counter

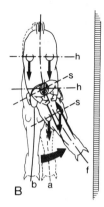

Figure 19: **A** = *Faulty execution of the shoulder-in with bend only in the neck;* **B** = *Correct counter shoulder-in; (h) Hips and (s) shoulders of horse and rider parallel. Note; a = Position of young and/or partly trained horse in relation to the wall; b = Position of the straightened horse; e = Shoulder-in position; f = Counter shoulder-in position.*

shoulder-in with the moderate degree of bending recommended above, one can practice the exercise on the circle. This is rarely done nowadays for reasons which it would take too long to explain, but by neglecting this lesson one deprives oneself of a singularly effective way of improving the animal's suppleness and his obedience to the leg. The old *Directives of the Spanish Riding School of Vienna* stated that the shoulder-in could be practiced on the large circle or along the wall, and especially recommended the practice of the movement on the circle.

In the next progressive stage the movement can be executed along the short sides of the arena; this naturally implies greater bend in the corners which are then ridden as a fraction of a volte.

There are significant differences between the shoulder-in and the counter shoulder-in on the circle. In the shoulder-in, the hindquarters follow the longer track and the inside hind of the horse and inside leg of the rider must be especially active; the outside leg must allow the horse's hindquarters sufficient freedom of movement and yet must prevent their swinging out. The coordination of aids requires a considerable measure of skill.

In the counter shoulder-in, the horse has to elevate the forehand rather more because the hindquarters must follow the shorter track. The outside rein is the bending rein as well as the collecting one, and the horse must go well up to the outside hand. For these reasons, the counter shoulder-in on the circle is particularly favorable to the development of collection.

Finally, the shoulder-in must be practiced away from the wall on the inside track and then on the centerline to verify that the horse can maintain direction unwaveringly when he is deprived of the balancing support of the wall.

The best way to improve the shoulder-in is to combine it with voltes at frequent intervals. If one feels that the bend is insufficient at the beginning of the shoulder-in, a correct course is to execute one or more voltes. If the bend diminishes or if a certain sluggishness is detected during the course of the movement, by executing a volte on a single track that position and liveliness are best restored.

If the rider concentrates his attention too much on the lateral movement and not enough on the forward movement, he risks neglecting to urge the horse forward as he must to maintain collection and prevent the horse trailing his hind limbs. If the rider fails to do so, the horse's outside hind ceases to step forward sufficiently, his outline becomes too long, the tension of the outside rein too slack; the collection progressively diminishes until eventually self-carriage is lost and the weight unsupported by the hind limbs is thrown onto the rider's hand.

Whenever one feels that the hind limbs are starting to disengage and to slacken, the best procedure is to ride forwards energetically toward the center of the arena until impulsion is restored and only then resume the lateral movement on the new track.

In the case of lazy horses it can be helpful to execute the movement in stages: beginning the shoulder-in on the long side at the usual starting place, then, after 10 to 15 meters, with the predominant aid of the outside leg, driving the horse onto the quarter line (between the wall and the centerline), there to execute a few more steps in shoulder-in and again to driving forwards onto the centerline, and so on until the opposite long side is reached.

To conclude this discussion of the shoulder-in, it remains to be said that in its usual form, that is, when three tracks are marked on the ground by the horse's hooves, it is a movement which unlike some others does not require special aptitude. It can be performed by any horse that can justifiably be called a saddle horse, provided that the movement is not introduced to the horse prematurely, that the rider is knowledgeable and sympathetic, that the difficulties are very gradually increased, and that the gait remains lively throughout the execution.

In the more advanced tests it can also be performed at the canter. One may wonder why this has not yet been required since it is an excellent preparation for the canter half pass and the pirouettes. All unschooled horses tend to move with the quarters in, especially at the canter because the somewhat crooked position facilitates this gait. The shoulder-in is therefore an excellent means of completing the task of straightening the horse and improving suppleness at the canter. However, one should remember that the shoulder-in position impedes the canter and an angle of 30 degrees is therefore the maximum that can be demanded; beyond this the purity of the gait would be destroyed.

The counter shoulder-in at canter is particularly useful with horses that stubbornly refuse to engage the inside hind in the counter-canter, especially in the turns. It is an evasion that is extremely difficult to correct when it has become a well-established habit. Straightness of the canter can be considered to have been achieved only when it is possible to control the inside hind in all changes of direction.

Finally, let us consider how we can eventually use the shoulder-in as a preparation for the half pass. Normally in the shoulder-in one displaces the forehand onto a track parallel to the one followed by the hindquarters and then continues to direct the horse forward on the original course in shoulder-in position. It is in this manner that it must be executed in tests and therefore also in this manner that it is usually practiced. However, it is useful occasionally in the course of the daily lessons to do the opposite, that is, to use the outside leg to bring the hindquarters in line with the forehand and then to continue riding on the inside track upon which the forehand was previously placed. This greatly helps to maintain the softness of the contact with the inside hand.

Chapter 8

Travers and Renvers

There are many misconceptions about travers and renvers, so it pays to set forth and discuss several fundamental differences. We will look at renvers and travers separately.

Travers and half pass are related movements. Let's compare the FEI definitions in the *Rules for Dressage Competitions*:

"Travers (head to the wall). The horse is lightly bent around the inner thigh of the rider. The outer hooves cross in front of and over the inner hooves. The horse looks in the direction of his movement. Execution of the travers is along the wall or better on the centerline, with an angle of bend of 30 degrees in the direction of his movement" (Figure 20).

The definition of the half pass (Art. 412.8) reads:

"Half pass. This is a variation of the travers, that should be executed on the diagonal instead of on the wall. The horse should be lightly bent around the inner thigh of the rider, in order to allow the shoulder more movement and through that give lesson lightness and elegance. The outer hooves should step in front of and over the inner hooves. The horse is looking in the direction that he is moving in. During the entire movement he should maintain the same rhythm and position."

When this paragraph says: "The half pass is a variation of the travers," it means that the half pass should be ridden on lines other than the travers; according to FEI competition rules, travers is ridden always along the wall or parallel to the wall, for example, on the centerline, whereas the half pass should be ridden on diagonal lines. In the execution itself there is no difference.

During everyday work the travers can also be practiced, of course, on curved lines (in turns or on the circle), and the half pass on any possible diagonal line, without changing the fundamentals of the lesson.

An example of this would be a half pass from the middle of one long side to the opposite middle of the other long side of the arena. One turns from the long side at B or E on a twenty meter circle and when during the turn the horse has the angle of bend of 30 degrees to the diagonal line and reaches the middle line, ride him on through a strengthening of the outside aids with an inwardly-pointing croup on two tracks. Shortly before reaching the other wall the lateral movement is ended and the horse turned onto one track (Figure 21).

Now for the distinctive features of the travers as opposed to the

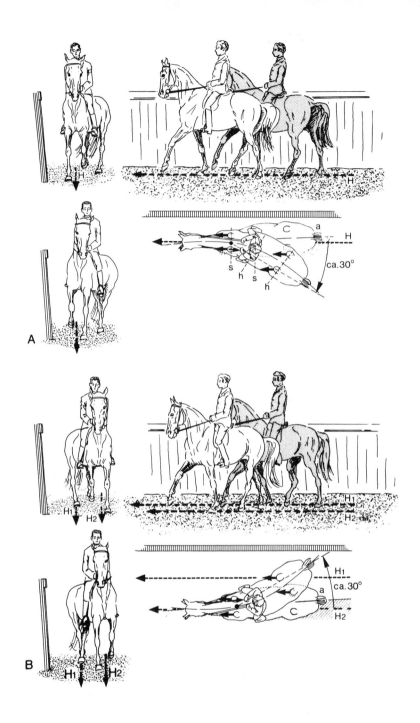

Figure 20: **A** = *Travers left at the trot (viewed from above, from the side and the front);* **B** = *Renvers right at the trot (viewed from above, from the side and the front).* **H** = *Track;* **H 1** = *Outer track;* **H 2** *Inner track.* **h** = *Horse's hips, rider's hips;* **s** = *Horse's shoulders, riders shoulders.*

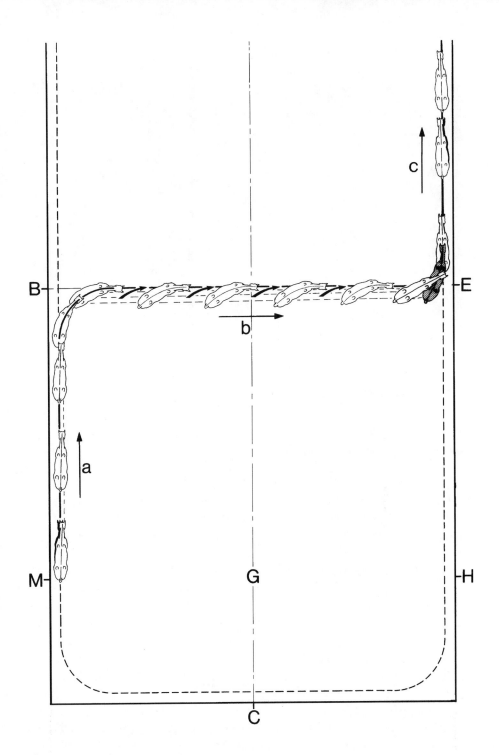

Figure 21: *Half pass from* **B** *to* **E**

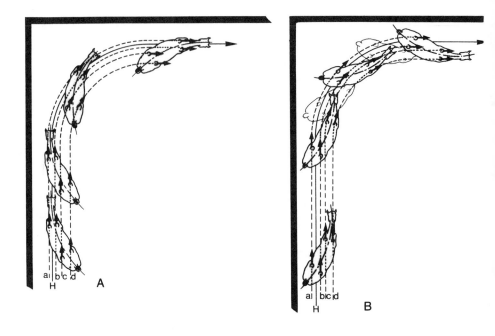

Figure 22: **A** = *Turning the corner in travers, at an angle of 30 degrees relative to the track.* **H** = *Track.* **a** = *Outside forefoot;* **b** = *Inside forefoot;* **c** = *Outside hind foot;* **d** = *Inside hind foot. Note that in travers the hind feet tread the shorter path and therefore have to be more loaded.*

22 **B** = *Turning the corner in renvers at an angle of 30 degrees with the track.* **H** = *Track.* **a** = *Inside hind foot;* **b** = *Outside hind foot;* **c** = *Inside forefoot;* **d** = *Outside forefoot. Note that on curved lines the hind feet tread the longer path, and that this makes collection more difficult.*

shoulder-in. The bend of the body is the same, but in travers the forehand goes almost straight and the hindquarters are placed to the inside. As a result, the horse mainly steps with the outer hind leg over and is then, in addition, affected by the outer aids of the rider. The movement is in the direction of his bend. So much for the differences between lessons on straight lines!

In turns and curved lines the hind legs have the shorter path in travers, and so they are more burdened. Therefore, turns in travers are more exhausting for the horse than the shoulder-in because it requires stronger collection. The increase in demand in travers as opposed to the shoulder-in comes best by first practicing in turns and on curved lines. So one should ride the lesson also on a 20 meter square (half of a 20 x

40 arena), and make sure that in all turns routinely following each other the main points of the lesson are fulfilled, especially the flow of the movement on the more burdened hindquarters.

The inwardly placed hindquarters is the least demand in this exercise; the majority of horses tend from nature to do this anyway, at least on one side. The main difficulty is to preserve the correct bend in inner side. This task falls for the most part to the rider's inner thigh, the meaning of which is often underestimated in travers. The inside rein sees to it that the head position is in the direction of the movement so that the edge of the forehead shows. The outside rein holds the position, leading the forehand and supporting the outside leg.

Many riders see the travers and especially the half pass as an exercise to gymnasticize the outside hind leg. In fact, however, the inner hind leg has to carry the burden, bending itself markedly more and because of that doing more work. This is also the reason why many horses, after having learned the inward position of the croup, are inclined to place the hind leg too far sideways and, as a result of that, burden and bend it less.

In travers whether just the outside hind leg or both outside legs cross over depends on the degree of the body bend. The more severe the body bend, the more the hindquarters are positioned to the inside while the forehand approaches going straight. The outside hind leg must, therefore, cross over the inside; the outside foreleg will now be in front of the inside, but not be placed farther over this way. It is analogous to the work of the hind leg in the shoulder-in, with which the inner hind leg steps in front of the outside, but whose path doesn't cross. The smaller the bend, the easier the simultaneous crossing over in back and in front is to the horse. That is especially observable in leg-yielding.

In the canter half pass, the crossing over is considerably more difficult because throughout the changed course of movement, following in three suspended phases rather than two, the outside legs lift up earlier than the inside legs and so can be placed no more sideways over the inside legs. A crossing over is therefore only possible during the suspended phase.

Additionally, one starts the travers, like all lateral movements, with slight bend and increases it over the course of the education.

With advanced horses, the lateral movements are also ridden at the canter. One can observe a timidity of the canter half pass with many otherwise completely experienced riders. It is understandable if one remembers that in the beginning of riding education the horse liked to move his croup inward and go crookedly, and that it took the rider a lot of effort to make the horse go straight and forward at the canter and the counter-canter. Later, though, this stage should be over, for at this point one should expect a straight horse on all straight lines and in all gaits, and a nicely bent horse on all corners and circles. One considers the transitions and lessons required in Second Level (tight turns, counter-canter, simple change of lead, and rein back, etc.) as the development of the scale from collected until extended trot, so it becomes clear that often more than half of all competitors in this class have started it too early. The equestrian experience confirms this assertion again and again. Jumping from First Level to Second Level is a much greater leap than many riders think. Many times there are difficulties in the higher class levels because the horse or rider concerned doesn't have enough of the basics of Second Level down pat. This is an omission that is harder and harder to make up for the older a horse and rider become.

The lateral movements at the canter should also be built into the training sessions by the beginning of very small lateral bends, all of this as soon as the horse has learned to keep his hind foot in the same track as the front foot and, through that, to bend sufficiently in transitions into the canter. These very small bends should be more than enough. Also, by the perfectly positioned lateral movement of the canter, the bend is somewhat smaller than at the trot and reaches its maximum on three tracks (Figure 24).

Neither canter half passes nor, later, half and full canter pirouettes can be developed cleanly without the canter work on two tracks on the wall.

Of course, one must watch his horse very carefully in the canter half pass and return to cantering on one track and shoulder-in canter if the horse falls out on the shoulder (from which the falling out of the hindquarters at the canter half pass originates) and thereby takes the burden off the inside hind foot. This point can be observed with travers and renvers at all gaits. Horses figure out very quickly how to unburden the inside hind by bending incorrectly at the withers or bending too much in the flank vertebrae so to place their hind legs too far sideways and thereby unburden the inside hind leg. To avoid this mistake, one must apply the outside leg no more than is just necessary to reach the required position. The inside aids check the softness of the inside and the track of the inner hind foot. If the inside hind foot runs away sideways in the half pass, by which the horse slides out (that means steps too far sideways, and because of that too reaches the wall too early), one applies the inside leg in the transition phase more than the outside one to correctly preserve the half pass.

Also, the travers and half pass are exercises for the inside hind foot, even if at first glance it doesn't look that way, because with the

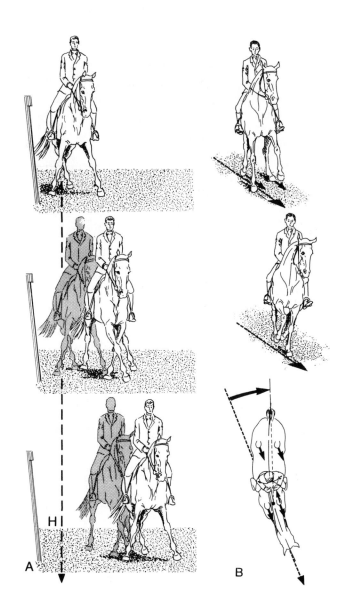

Figure 23: **A** = *Left half pass with very marked over-stepping of the outside hind.*
B = *Left half pass at canter on the long diagonal of an arena of 20 x 60 m. Angle of positioning of approximately 20 degrees (the horse parallel to the long side).* **H** = *Outer track.*

outside aids one causes the outside hind foot to cross over and the outside hind foot takes advantage of it. The inside hind foot must step in the direction of the burden, supporting and lightly bending if the

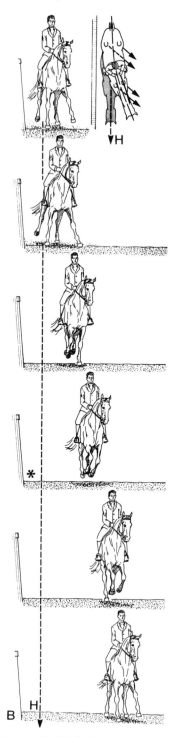

Figure 24: *Successive phases of a left half pass at canter. Note that to make room for the outside hind, track* **H** *is not against the wall.* * = *Period of suspension;* **B** = *Wall of the arena.*

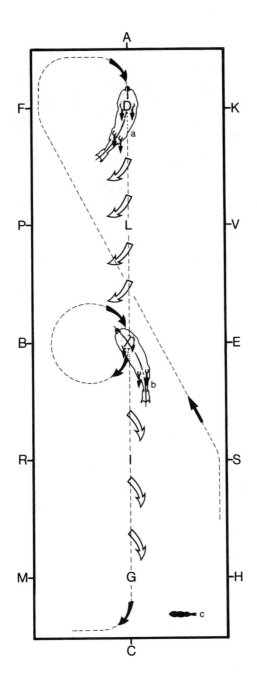

Figure 25: *Right shoulder-in on the centerline;* **b** = *Volte at X followed by renvers on the centerline;* **c** = *Actual size of the horse in relation to the arena.*

exercise is to fulfill its purpose. Therefore, it is its releasing sideways that is normally one of the biggest mistakes that could ever occur in this lesson. "Normally" should mean that there are also horses for whom the half pass is very hard. They require lasting aids, and if it occurs through these aids that the hindquarters goes too far to the wall or the hindquarters in the half pass falls out, then the damage is not all that important for a correct lateral movement through softening of the a to reach it is always easier than to have to "create" it through extraordinarily strong aids. In order to correct the mistake of the falling out quarters or to not let it happen at all, we like to ride (named by us) "step half passes." One starts in shoulder-in, and after several steps puts the horse with the outside leg into the half pass, presses after a few meters with the inside leg once again into the shoulder-in and so on, as long as the measurements of the arena allow. This exercise improves both lessons, for the horse in the shoulder-in may neither fall out with the outside hind foot or go ahead with the hindquarters moving sideways (otherwise the half pass can't go forward).

In the art of classical riding, only the goals are unchangeable. The paths are ordered but in keeping with the direction, the individual nature of each horse requires certain modifications. Therefore, it can't be said which mistakes within a certain lesson are the greater or lesser mistakes. If a horse goes, for example, by nature on his forehand, then temporary extreme aids represent a smaller mistake than the yielding downwards. A horse that is constantly above the bit behaves the opposite way. Therefore, one should always just say: "with this particular horse, this mistake is more or less serious."

The counter lesson to travers is called renvers. The FEI requirements describe this lateral movement briefly but comprehensively:

"Renvers (tail to the wall). This is the opposite position to travers, with the tail at the position of the head to the wall. Incidentally, renvers shall be executed according to the same fundamentals and the same conditions as travers"

As long as one rides on straight lines, the aids are the same, only the softness of the inside side must be paid even more attention. Straight riding without walls results in no difference for the horse if the lateral movement in this case is called travers or renvers; it just depends on if one draws the borderlines in front of or behind the horse.

Things look completely different, however, in turns and on curved lines. Here things reverse themselves. In renvers, the hindquarters are just as heavily burdened as in travers, but they have to take the longer path in turns. This requires even more application on the part of the rider as well as powerful work for the sides of the horse. In addition to that, the sideways movement of the hindquarters runs the opposite of the bend. Therein lies the special ingredient of this exercise that in practice, unfortunately, is used much too infrequently.

A circle in renvers position makes it unclear to the horse what it means to take the hindquarters along at each step. The forehand remains on the inner, smaller circle and will be maintained on this circle primarily through the outside rein. One gains as a result of that a drastic means of bringing the horse increasingly on the outside rein in the opposite lessons in general and especially in renvers. In his work *The Art of Classical Riding,* Podhajsky characterized, for example, the renvers-volte as an "excellent suppleness exercise," which it is. But one has to either go far or wait long to see it somewhere. What is the cause of that? This exercise is out of the question for average riders. Advanced dressage riders and competitors are almost exclusively busy with the lessons that occur in the individual dressage tests. Admittedly, these are difficult enough. In order to reach a certain goal, one sometimes needs completion and improvement possibilities (in strategy, additional measures). To that end, the renvers is well-suited on curved lines. The renvers will be nearly unavoidable, however, in the preparation and development of canter-pirouettes as we shall see the discussion of that lesson.

In renvers it is even more difficult to control the skill and bend of the inner hind foot. If this is successful, then the horse will turn more softly to the inner, curved side than to the outer side. So, for example, out of the renvers a volte to the right is more easy to execute than to the left.

There is a tendency with lateral movements to never leave the straight line. It is probably because it is not demanded in dressage tests. But if one wants to achieve the complete gymnastic effect, then one must practice lateral movements on curved lines.

The execution is more difficult and places increased demands on the ability of rider and horse, but is more profitable and one can only make oneself undertake this effort. First, on these lines come the criteria and the special use of the various lateral movements for the carrying of weight. The increased effort in the turns makes horses much more industrious and secure on straight lines, because after exertion on curved lines the exertion on straight lines is much easier.

The advice "renvers right" or "renvers left" for other lines than the outside wall sometimes causes confusion.

To say it as simply as possible, the indication right or left with lateral movements depends neither on the direction nor the hand that

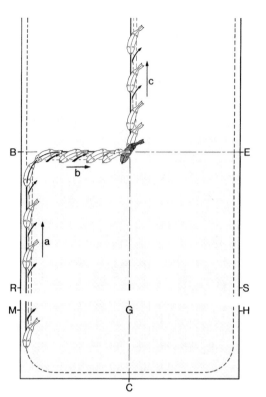

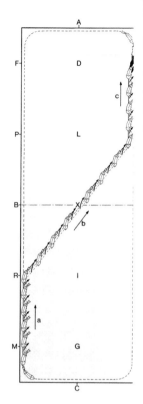

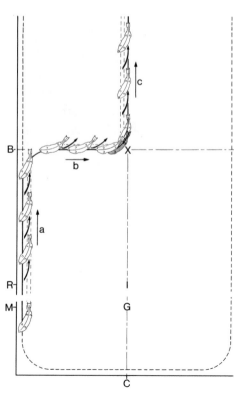

Figure 26:

A = Shoulder-in - Travers - Shoulder-in

B = Shoulder-in - Half pass - Counter Shoulder-in

C = Renvers - Shoulder-in - Travers

Figure 27: *Which exercises are being performed here? It depends exclusively on the direction of the movement and the line taken.*

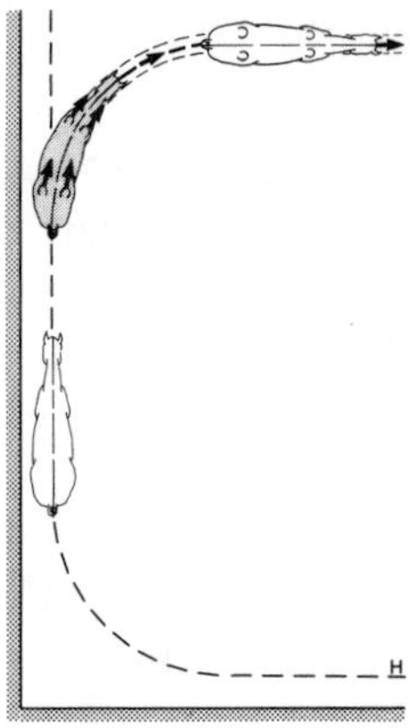

a) A turn
(H = Track

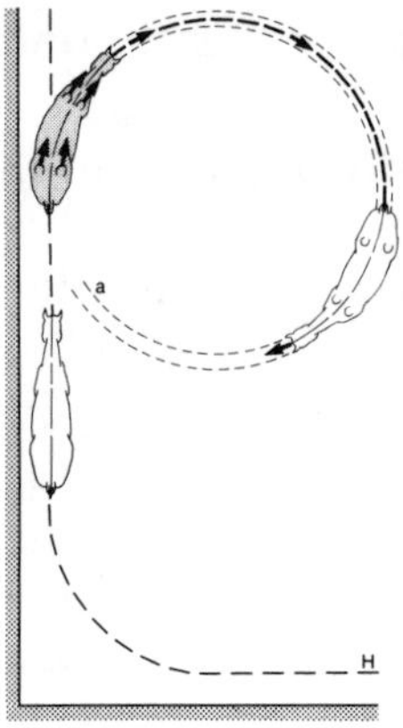

b) A volte
(H = Track

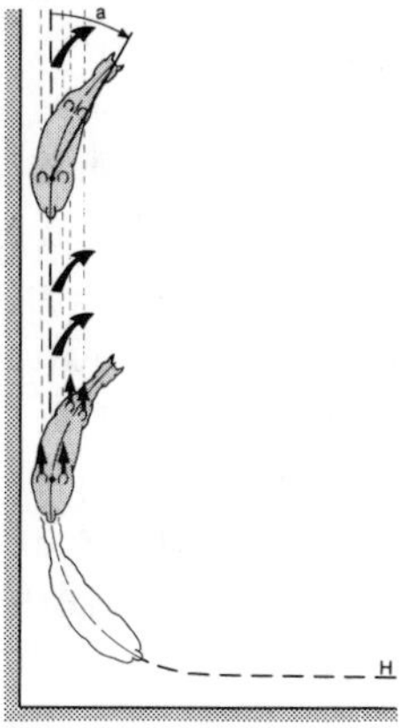

c) Shoulder-in
(H = Track; a =
Angle of 30 degrees)

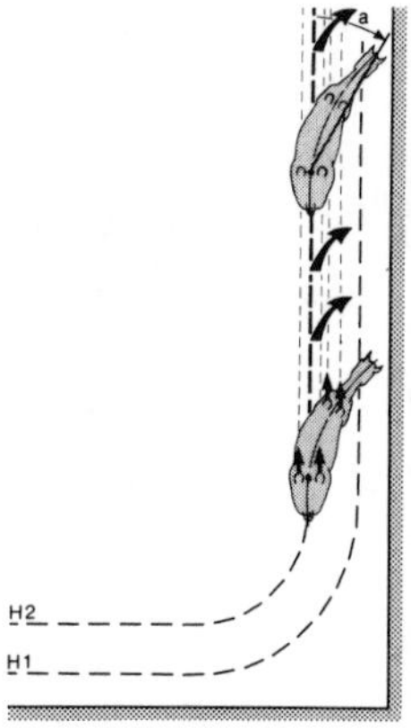

d) Counter shoulder-in
(H1 = Track, H2 = Inner
or second track; a =
Angle of 30 degrees)

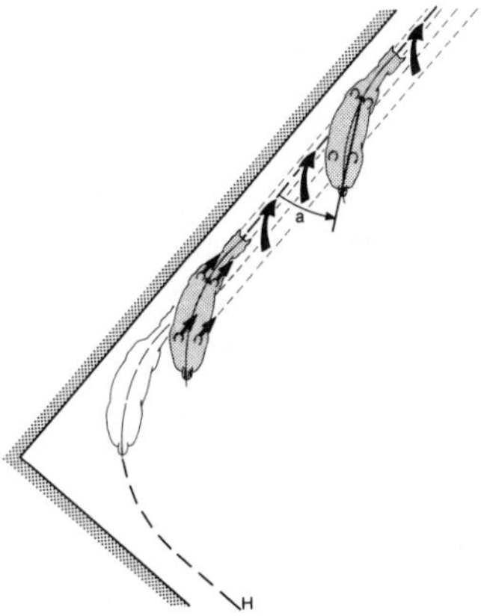

e) Travers
(H = Track; a =
Angle of 30 degrees)

f) Half pass
(H = Track; a =
angle of 30 degrees;
b = Line of movement)

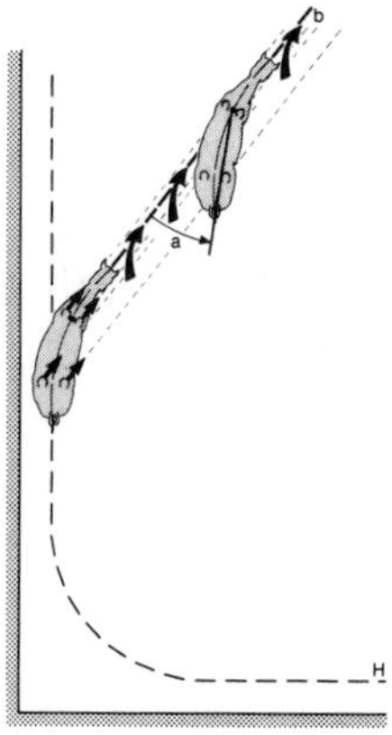

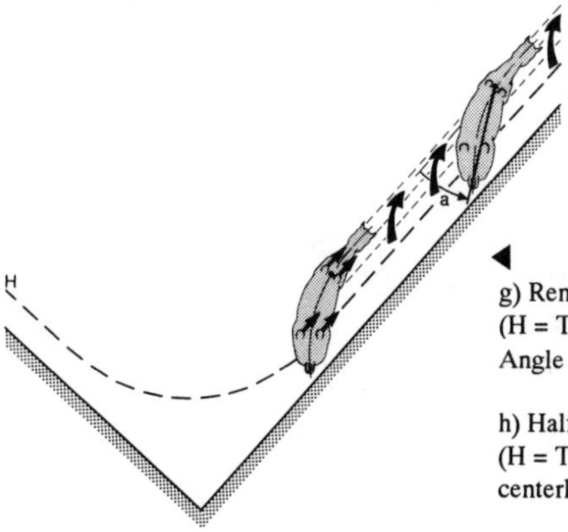

g) Renvers
(H = Track; a =
Angle of 30 degrees)

h) Half or full pirouette,
(H = Track, a = On the
centerline with change of rein

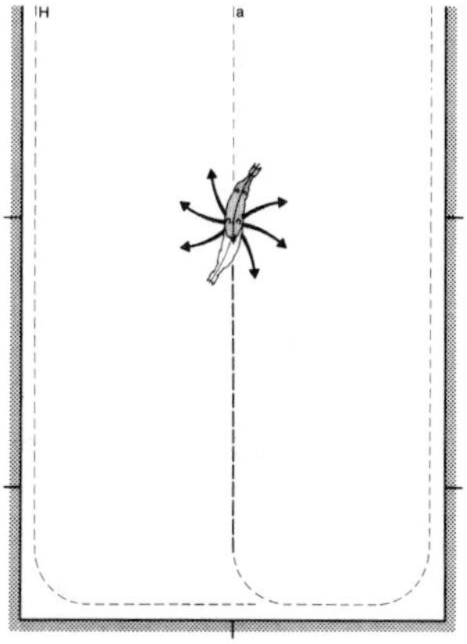

87

one is on, but instead solely and alone from the bend of the horse. The manner of the lateral movement is determined by the bend and arena walls. In shoulder-in and travers the front legs remain on the wall. Shoulder-in and travers to the right can be done only on the right hand, counter shoulder-in and renvers to the right only on the left hand and vice versa.

These confusions can only originate in the previous chapter on counter shoulder-in and renvers. This is most likely because several specialty books call the renvers on the left hand "renvers right" ("renvers the left way around" is meant) and name the right "renvers left." That is however, not in the mind of the inventor, for with renvers on the left hand the horse must be bent to the right and vice versa. In practice it is not at all necessary to say "right" or "left," for the educated rider the indication "renvers" is enough and the execution will be obvious. According to de la Gueriniere, renvers on the right hand is very clearly named "renvers left," and on the left side "renvers right."

If it says, for example, on the centerline, coming from A: "At X volte right and renvers right," then after the end of the volte the forehand of the horse will be led out from the centerline, still in right bend, and the hind legs remain on the centerline. At G the horse straightens himself and at C takes up the right hand. Every other execution cannot be considered correct.

At Third Level and above, absolute precision should be mastered at the lateral movements. It may happen that individual riders aren't completely confident with these concepts and contexts. Since long discussion about this occurs frequently among trainers of dressage, riding instructors, judges of dressage and other specialists, let all participants pay special heed!

In the new FEI tests, renvers no longer appears. It is a shame that such an interesting, educational exercise is no longer in any international dressage test.

The transitions from one lateral movement to the other is a great help in the daily work of the advanced dressage horse. Figure 26 demonstrates how several lateral movements without change of the bend allow themselves to be connected simply by the change of direction.

According to the side of the horse that is more difficult, there are suitable possibilities of combinations for each case.

For the conclusion of the chapter on lateral movements there is one more interesting summary; see Figure 27.

Chapter 9

The Counter-Canter

In the context of our discussion, we need not concern ourselves with the question of whether the counter-canter is a movement that is natural to the horse. In any case, apart from movements that animals instinctively learn for the sake of survival, what are the ones that can be called natural? Is labor natural to man? Was the horse created to carry a rider? Should all activity that requires a measure of effort be deemed unnatural? Are the lateral movements, especially travers, natural? And what about the rein back?

The fact is that as a gait the counter-canter is of no utilitarian value. It is purely gymnastic work—like all dressage exercises—designed to improve the maneuverability of the horse. In this respect, its unquestionable advantages were recognized many hundreds of years ago, and it has for that reason become firmly established in our system of training and in the FEI tests.

Of what particular advantage then is the counter-canter compared to other work at canter?

Nobody denies the necessity of teaching horses to move straight when loaded with the weight of a rider, especially at the canter. For this purpose, the counter-canter is of invaluable assistance. Since the inside of the horse is then turned towards the wall of the arena, the sideways evasion of the inside hind, often so difficult to prevent in true canter, is more difficult. That is provided, of course, the movement is correctly ridden, with the horse's inside shoulder closer to the wall than his inside hip, much as in the counter shoulder-in (Figure 28 A and B).

It is this position, which must be carefully maintained especially in the corners, that deprives the horse of the possibility of cantering crookedly by turning his hindquarters in. The rider's outside leg (relative to position) counters any tendency to turn the quarters out.

When the counter-canter is executed along the wall, the outside rein can be more effectively used to keep the neck straight since the presence of the wall helps obviate the evasion of the hindquarters which most horses resort to in true canter in order to avoid uncomfortable flexion of the inside hind.

Besides this, the counter-canter is also used to improve collection. This, in fact, is its principal purpose.

It is known that collection cannot be enhanced unless one can succeed in shortening the convex side of the horse. In the counter-canter

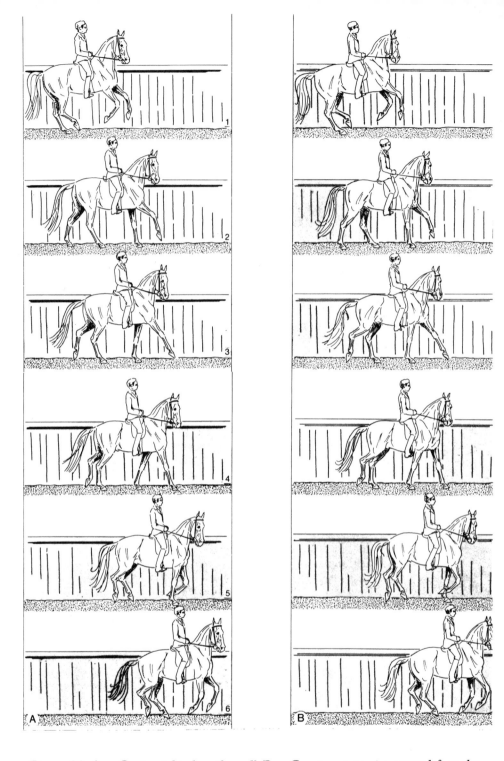

Figure 28: **A** = *Canter right along the wall;* **B** = *Counter-canter, i.e. canter left on the right rein.*

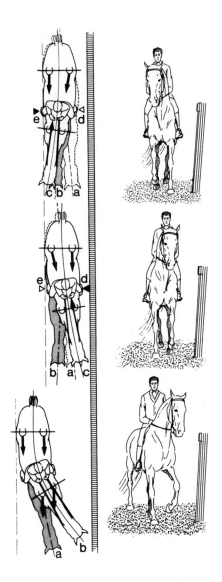

Figure 29: *Above, true canter right.* **a** = *Natural position of unstraightened horse;* **b** = *Straightened horse;* **c** = *Position of horse in true canter;* **d** = *Outer, guarding leg of rider;* **e** = *Inside, forward impelling leg of rider. Center, left counter-canter.* **a** = *Natural crookedness of the horse;* **b** = *Horse straightened before the transition to counter-canter;* **c** = *Position of the horse in counter-canter;* **d** = *Inside, impelling leg of the rider in counter-canter (outside leg in true canter);* **e** = *Outside, guarding leg in counter-canter (inside leg in true canter). Below,* **a** = *Position of horse in counter-canter;* **b** = *Compare with position in counter shoulder-in.*

as the hind quarter is turned outwards when turning, the task of the outside rein becomes much facilitated.

The constant effect of the outside rein, combined with the more positive effect of the outside leg which must impel the outside hind to engage exactly in the direction of the outside rein, forces the horse willy-nilly to move more collectedly. Or better said, the horse collects himself since he cannot turn without, at every spring of the canter, meeting the steadily maintained tension of the outside rein. The rider must, of course, drive forward effectively to maintain the briskness of the movement and thus prevent disengagement behind. The desired measure of collection, depending on the intensity of the aids, should ensue almost automatically.

The counter-canter, which was invented, practiced and developed by the creative riding masters of the past, has never failed in its purpose when used with tact and understanding.

In all counter-canter figures the horse must remain bent in the direction of the leading forefoot, and both the rider's legs must ensure that the hind feet following the track of the forefeet. If the movement is viewed from the front, the inside forefoot must conceal the inside hind foot and the outside hind foot should be visible between the forefeet (Figure 29).

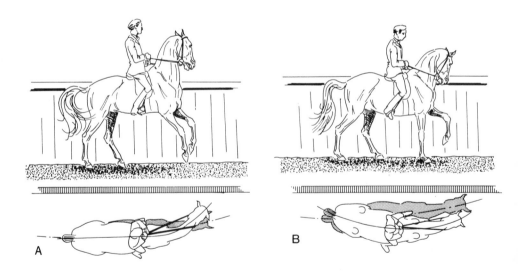

Figure 30: *Faulty counter-canter.* **A** = *Active elevation of the neck, hollowing of the back, impure sequence of footfalls.* **B** = *Excessively restraining hands, horse overbent, canter over-shortened.*

Exaggerated pressure of the outside leg would cause the horse to move on two tracks, in a renvers-like position; this is a very serious fault. Bending the horse too much, that is, bending mostly the neck to force the counter-canter before the horse is ready for the exercise, is an equally serious fault. The worst fault, however, and one to which most horses are inclined in the beginning because of the initial difficulty of the counter-canter, is an alteration of the pace. The horse either hurries or, as is more likely, loses speed and canters four-time. To avoid this fault, from the very introduction of the exercise, it is absolutely necessary to preserve impulsion with the inside leg, especially on curves or corners. Moreover it is most unwise to try to shorten the stride by excessive use of hands since very few horses are capable of cantering with unimpaired impulsion when the forehand is excessively elevated. And very few riders have the power to drive with the force and effectiveness required to counteract with the legs the elevating effect of the hands, thus preserving the springiness of the gait.

Inept shortening of the canter produces a movement which can most flatteringly be described as "canter-like," in which the spring is entirely lost, the hind limbs partly hopping, partly trailing behind in a sort of trot-like motion.

Many riders wonder when they can start teaching the horse to counter-canter. The answer is that several conditions must be fulfilled for the movement to conform to the rules of classical dressage.

To begin with, the horse must have learned to canter true, in horizontal equilibrium, on all the figures required in novice and elementary tests. The working canter should have become really active and perfectly regular, and it should be possible occasionally to obtain a few slightly collected strides. Correct execution at what can be described as an active, lightly shortened working canter of the figures illustrated in Figure 31 involving turns requiring a degree of bend of the second degree would be a good test of sufficient submission and suppleness. If the horse remains calm, secure and regular in turns and on straight lines to both hands, the rider may safely ask for a change of hand using counter-canter.

The counter-canter, in fact, should not cause any problem if the horse has been well prepared in work at the true canter. If an experienced horse is not capable of executing counter-canter without loss of poise, it demonstrates the horse is not properly balanced and regular true canter either, and loses his poise and balance when turning through corners and on curves or voltes of a diameter of 8 m. It is then a case of going back as far as necessary to basic education.

Regarding progression, one must start with the easiest exercise,

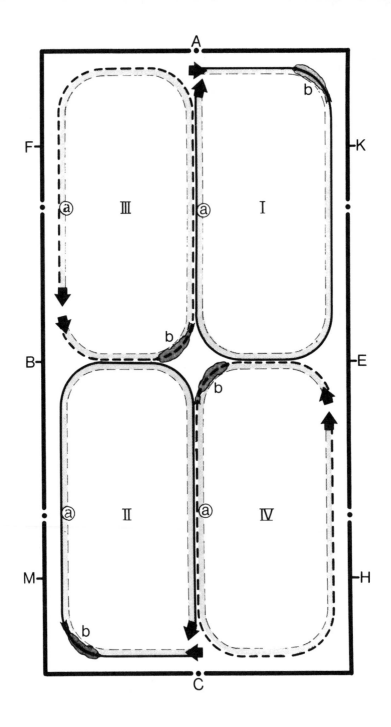

Figure 31: *An arena figure which tests a horse's readiness to start work in counter-canter. I, II, III, IV = each equal in size to a quarter of an arena of 20 x 40 m.* **a** = *Inner side of the horse;* **b** = *Horse cantering true.*

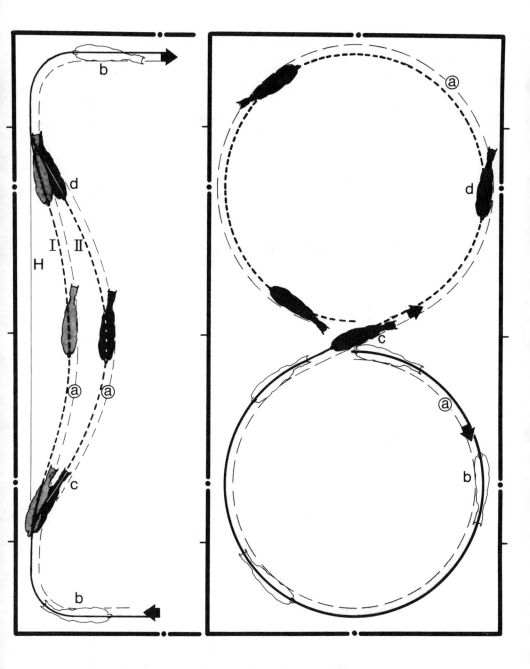

Figure 32 (left): *First stage of work on counter-canter.* **H** = *Track.* **I** = *Shallow arc of a circle (no more than 2.50 m from track).* **II** = *Arc of a slightly smaller circle (up to 5 m from track).* **a, b** = *True canter;* **c, d** = *Counter-canter.*

Figure 33 (right): *Figure eight without change of lead.* **a** = *Inside of horse;* **b** = *True canter;* **c** = *Change of hand without change of lead;* **d** = *Counter-canter.*

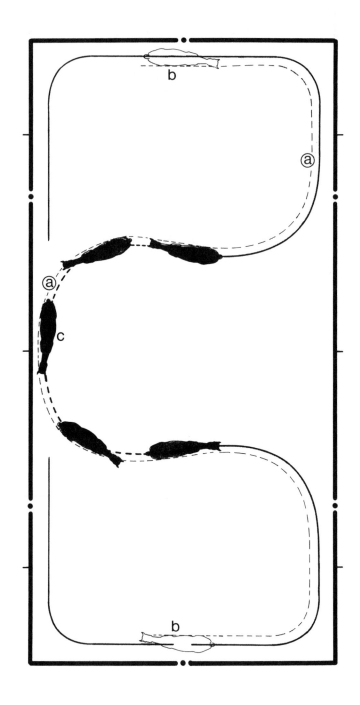

Figure 34: *Serpentine of three loops without change of lead.* **a** = *Inside of horse;* **b** = *True canter;* **c** = *Counter-canter.*

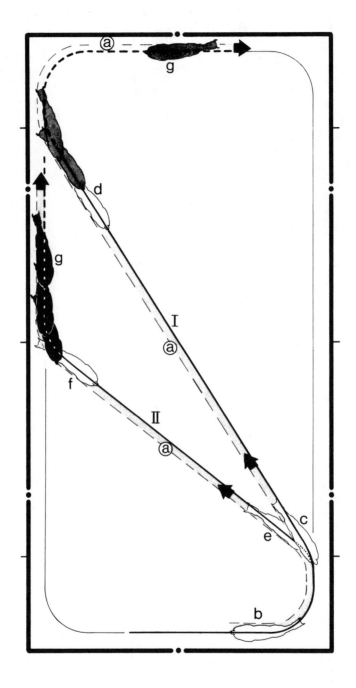

Figure 35: *Change of hand across the entire or the half-arena.* **I** = *On the long diagonal;* **II** = *On the short diagonal; a* = *Inside of horse; b, c* = *True canter into counter-canter at* **d**; **b-e** = *True canter into counter-canter at* **f**.

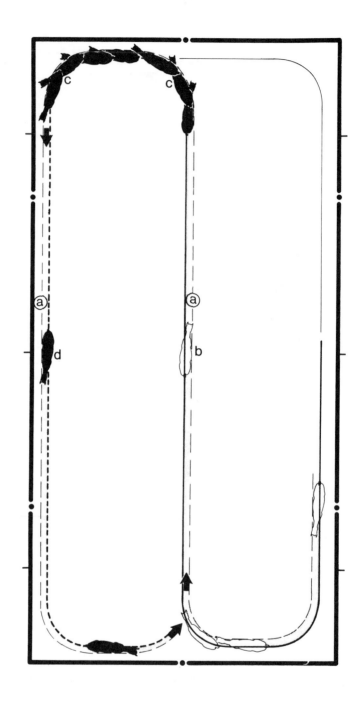

Figure 36: *Change of hand on the centerline.* **a** = *Inside of horse;* **b** = *True canter;* **c,** **d** = *counter-canter.*

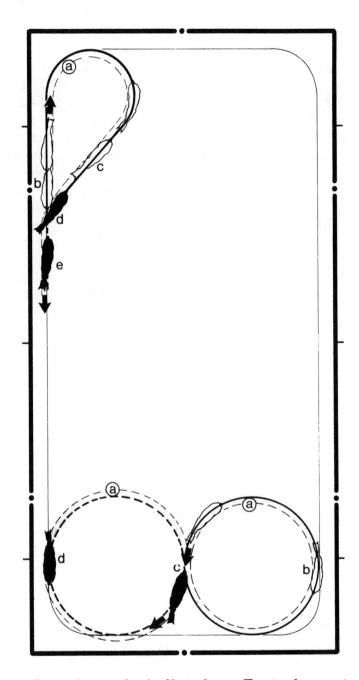

Figure 37: *Above: Demi-volte.* **a** = *Inside of horse;* **b**, **c** = *Turning the corner in true canter;* **d**, **e** = *Counter-canter. Below: Testing the horse's proficiency at counter-canter, figure eight on the short side of the arena without changing lead.* **a** = *Inside of the horse;* **b** = *True canter;* **c** = *Change of hand towards the closed side of the arena without changing the lead;* **d** = *Counter-canter.*

which does not entail a change of hand. This is a very shallow loop on the long side, so shallow that the horse does not feel that he is in fact counter-cantering on the second part of the loop. If the horse has been properly prepared he will remain quite unperturbed. It may be possible, perhaps even in the course of the first lesson, to make the curve more pronounced. In any case, after no more than a few days it should be possible to execute the more pronounced change of direction with equal facility to both hands. After this, one can progress to the figure eight, and then to the complete circle and the serpentine. When these figures can be executed to both hands without any disturbance to the gait one may increase the difficulty gradually by executing the figures illustrated in Figures 36 and 37. Figure 37, however, is rather severely taxing.

It is, of course, impossible to state the length of time needed before one can progress from one form of the exercise to the next more difficult one. It depends entirely on the behavior of the horse. If he maintains calmness, regularity and unaltered equilibrium in the counter-canter, after one or two circles or turns one should go back to true canter. If, on the contrary, he starts to hurry or to lean on the hand, a transition to walk must be immediately executed to get the horse sufficiently collected. One then returns to a controlled true canter with a few turns and voltes to improve carriage and suppleness before once again with due prudence giving the horse a short and simple lesson in counter-canter. If he does well, he must immediately be praised and allowed to relax at the walk on a long rein.

It must be said that almost always when a horse hurries in counter-canter it is because an inexperienced rider in his efforts to prevent a change of lead, urges the horse on with exaggeratedly strong aids, especially with that of his outside leg, sits much too heavily, exaggerates the lateral weight effect or, alternately, sits to the wrong side.

Strong pressure of the outside leg is useless in preventing a break of the canter to the trot; on the contrary, it often provokes the break because it can result in forcing the horse to move on two tracks. A relatively uneducated horse cannot possibly remain in counter-canter on two tracks.

Leaning in the direction of the turn is equally detrimental. If for example, the horse is in right canter to the left hand (leading with the right fore and moving anti-clockwise), the rider must sit to the right, and it is the inside, right hind of the horse, rather than the left hind, that he must activate mostly. If the inside right hind steps outwards towards the outside of the turn (probably because of excessive pressure with the rider's left [outside] leg), the horse is given all liberty to disrupt the counter-canter. It is partly with the inside leg and partly with the reins that one prevents this from happening.

It has been pointed out that certain figures executed at true canter can demonstrate whether a horse is ready or not to learn the counter-canter. There are, also certain figures that demonstrate the adroitness of the horse in counter-canter. The figure eight without change of lead on the short side of the arena is just such an exercise.

One should start the figure in the second half of the short side in order to change direction towards the closed side of the arena. Both the voltes must be equally 10 m and perfectly circular; moreover, gait, collection and bend must remain correct during the entire execution of the movement (Figure 37).

The ability to perform several of such figures eight, as well to one hand as to the other, is proof indeed of a high degree of craftsmanship.

Chapter 10

Simple Changes and Flying Changes of Canter

In principle the simple change of canter can be executed, more or less easily, at any place in the arena and along any line. A transition to medium walk from working or collected canter is executed, the horse's position is then changed and after two or three strides of walk the new canter is started. The transition to walk must be immediate—without any intervening vaguely trot-like strides—but smooth. The steps must be determined and the four footfalls of the gait must be distinct; the transition to the new canter must also be immediate. The horse must canter straight, in horizontal equilibrium, and must constantly remain on the bit.

A perfect simple change (Figure 38) is not as easy to execute as some might think. It requires strong, supple, compliant hindquarters, capable of being considerably loaded. The horse must also allow himself to be flexed at the poll; insufficient flexibility of this region is sometimes the cause of the difficulty that may be experienced in obtaining a fluent transition from canter to walk, even if the horse offers no resistance to the hand in trot and canter. However, if the haunches are still too weak, in the transition to walk the horse stiffens them and throws his weight onto the forehand; their stiffness is evident in the transition to canter also. Difficulties in obtaining fluent simple changes originate more usually in the haunches than in the poll.

The best way of ensuring that the hind limbs are sufficiently engaged to permit a smooth transition from canter to walk is to execute it on the circle or, at a later stage, on a 10 m volte. To canter on a circle or a volte, the horse must lighten the forehand by flexing the haunches more than on straight lines, especially the inside hindquarter.

It is difficult to perform a good transition to walk on the straight. But to make the haunches more supple it is not sufficient to canter on a circle and occasionally demand the walk. On the contrary, transitions to walk and to canter must be frequently executed, and the periods of cantering must be short. If the horse stiffens in the transition to walk, the canter must not be resumed before the regularity of the walk on the circle or the volte, with correct bend, is established again. Once the exercise has been performed several times to one hand to the satisfaction of the rider, it is repeated to the other hand; more time

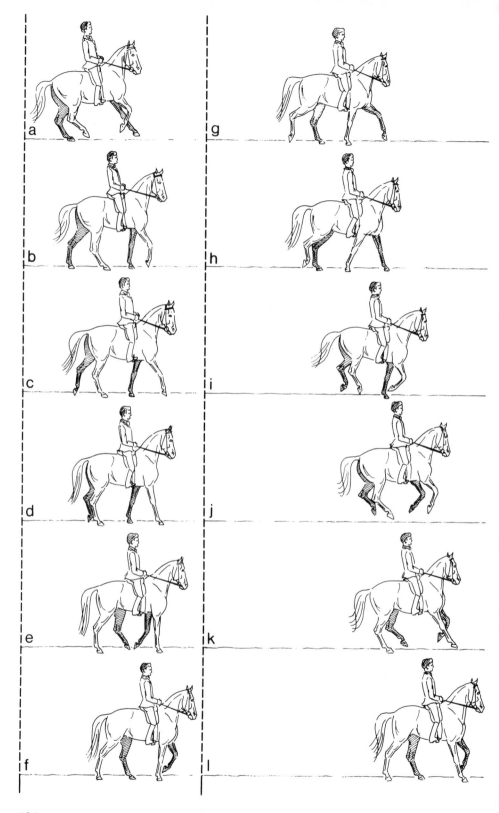

a

b

c

d

e

f

g

h

i

j

k

l

must, of course, be devoted to the difficult side (usually the right one).

When the transitions to walk and canter have become so fluent that the number of strides at the walk can be reduced to two or three, the transition to walk can be executed at the intersection of two circles just before a change of hand, the new canter is asked for as the horse's position is changed. At the beginning the number of intervening strides at walk is not the most important consideration; what matters most is the smoothness of the transition to walk and the quickness of the horse's reaction to the canter aids. This does not mean that the horse must leap up like a frog into the canter, but that he must respond promptly to the aids and canter onwards rather than upwards, calmly but with energy.

The exercise should be combined with work at counter-canter, with demi-volte, serpentines, change of hand on the diagonal or the short diagonal of the half-arena. For a long time, however, it is not advisable to practice the simple change on the straight, for example at the middle of the long side.

Simple changes on straight lines—on the inside track, or at X on the diagonal or on the centerline from A to C can be started when the change of canter with very few intervening steps at the walk has become perfectly fluent on the figure eight on the short side. Here, the walls of the arena greatly facilitate maintenance of straightness and poise in the canter. If riders need several strides of the walk before starting the new canter, it is often because they lack agility and their reactions are too slow. In the "transition" to walk, they painstakingly change their position before changing the position of the horse and then, with equal ponderousness, give the aids for canter; by this time the horse has had time to put in at least three strides at the walk. This deliberateness may be understandable during the first attempts at a simple change, but in order to perform the complex movement fluently one must learn to change one's position at the moment of executing the transition to walk and then give the indication to canter after no more than one or two strides of walk (the horse normally needs one more stride at the walk before his mind can register the command to canter).

The difficulty can be considerably enhanced by executing a simple change from counter-canter to counter-canter. This requires, of course, great responsiveness on the part of the horse and on the part of the rider rather more emphatic aids.

Figure 38: *Simple change of canter from right to left.* **a-c** = *Canter right;* **d-f** = *Transition to walk, 2-3 intervening steps at walk and change of position;* **g-l** = *Canter left.*

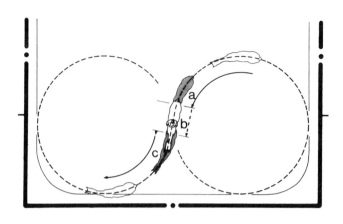

Figure 39: *Figure eight with simple change from left to right.* **a** = *Canter left and transition to walk;* **b** = *Walk;* **c** = *Canter right.*

Ultimate perfection is attained when one can ride the horse around the arena away from the wall, without changing hand, alternately at outside or inside canter (counter-or true canter) and execute a simple change after a predetermined number of strides of canter, though not necessarily consistently the same number. This is an exacting test of a horse's obedience. One can, for example, do a complete circuit of the arena alternately at true and counter-canter, changing canter every eight strides with three intervening strides at walk. Or do eight strides in right canter, four strides at the walk, seven strides in canter left, three strides of walk, six right center strides, two strides at walk, etc.

In a series of simple changes of canter conforming absolutely to the principles of classical equitation, the rider must be able to keep his horse straight, and constantly at the same distance from the outside track. As soon as the simple changes can be fluently executed with only one or two intervening strides of walk, the flying change can be taught without any fear of running into problems.

Flying changes must never be wrested from a horse before he can perform fluent simple changes by riding at an insane speed on the diagonal and throwing the frightened animal off balance in the corner with rough rein and weight effects. This is sometimes done by dealers to impress a gullible buyer trying to find a horse with which he will soon be able to compete in dressage competitions at medium level. The damage done in this way can hardly ever be repaired. A horse thus abused will always become extremely agitated when required to do a change of canter.

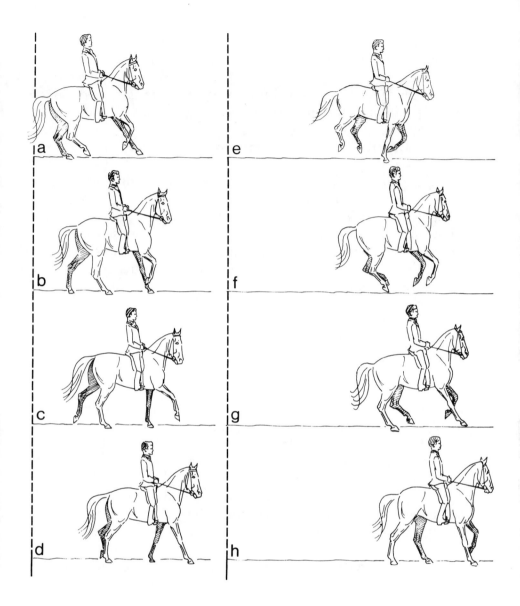

Figure 40: *Flying change from right to left.* **a-e** = *Right canter;* **e, f** = *Change of position;* **f** = *Change of lead at the moment of suspension;* **g, h** = *Left canter.*

The Flying Change

During the fairly long period of schooling necessary to teach the horse to counter-canter, he may often neatly change lead in mid-air in a turn rather than experience the difficulty of counter-cantering through a corner. In fact, the flying change unintended by the rider is frequently much more fluent than the ones which he subsequently tries to obtain in obedience to the conventional aids! This may show that the horse has a favorable aptitude for the change of canter, but it also shows that he changes perfectly fluently only when the decision to do so is his own. If at a later stage he does not react to the aids for the change or does not change correctly, it clearly demonstrates either that he does not yet understand the aids for canter, or does not wish to obey them at that particular moment.

A perceptive rider will either drive the horse firmly forwards in counter-canter when he feels it is about to change, or better still, will change his own position to accord with the change and ride the horse on calmly in the new canter. He must on no account punish the horse for doing something which he will eventually be asked to do.

But one must be prepared to devote an inordinately long period of time to the practice of the counter-canter. The habit of counter-canter must be confirmed to the extent that one's first attempts to get the horse to change lead in the air will mostly probably fail.

One should start to teach the flying change as soon as the horse feels perfectly balanced in counter-canter. "Never rush, but do not tarry" is the motto of the intelligent trainer.

Teaching a horse to execute a flying change should never be done before he can canter straight in perfect horizontal equilibrium, can be evenly bent on voltes to both hands, and is perfectly submissive to the aids. Horses vary so much in their aptitudes and disposition that it is impossible to say how long it may take to achieve this result, but it is certainly not attainable within a matter of weeks or months from the beginning of schooling. There are no prodigies in the equine species and even if there were some, it would be imprudent to let them discover how intelligent they are by teaching them too much too quickly!

One will always have to take into account the mental as well as the physical aptitudes of the horse for the flying change, which is one of the criteria—though not the only one—by which one can judge whether a horse is ready to perform successfully at the medium levels in dressage competitions. There are no aids which can force a horse to change lead in the air. The animal must have the right instinct for it and a cheerful disposition; neither are in the nature of phlegmatic horses. Natural bodily adroitness, and pure enjoyment of movement are essential ingredients of the recipe for the flying change. Clumsy though vigorous humans will always be incapable of surmounting their aversion to certain gymnastic exercises because an inner voice tells them not to make fools of themselves. Similarly, a horse cannot be a good prospect

108

for advanced dressage unless enough hot blood and zest for living is part of his system—though tranquility is nonetheless an equally desirable attribute. The strongest of riders can achieve nothing with an apathetic horse.

Herculean strength is not required to make an impression on a horse. An effective rider will be able to obtain better results than a weak one, but effectiveness is less a question of muscular power than of skill and experience. In any case there are limits to human strength. There are known cases of extremely capable and strong riders and trainers who have totally failed to obtain a correct flying change—or any of the difficult movements of the high school—from a particular horse. If it were all just a question of irresistible aids, an exceptionally strong rider could turn any horse into a proficient Grand Prix performer; unfortunately, or thank heavens, this is not the case.

Whether a horse is ready to be taught the change in the air depends principally on his proficiency at counter-canter and in simple changes. It must spontaneously canter straight and have become responsive to the lightest of aids.

Yet, however well-prepared a horse may be, one can expect a certain difficulty, unprecedented in previous canter lessons when teaching him to execute perfect flying changes. There are many well-known methods and a few not-well-known ones of overcoming the difficulty, any one of which may be appropriate to a particular case. Finding the right one is a matter of experience, feeling and, to some extent, of intuition. There is no standard recipe because every horse is an individual and we should always remember that what is good medicine for one person may kill another.

While the teaching of simple changes is based on an understanding of the mechanics of the horse, the teaching of the flying change is more a matter of artistic ability. It requires at least as much psychology as technical competence. By sticking stubbornly to a method which is unsuitable for a particular animal, one faces frustrating difficulty or even complete failure. The temperament and conformation of a horse, which both determine his manner of cantering, must therefore always be carefully considered before making a choice of method.

Always provided that the horse has been thoroughly prepared by work at counter-canter and on the simple changes, one can get him to execute a flying change either on a straight line or on a curve, or some special line of one's choosing or again make use of the wall of the arena. Collection may have to be increased, or on the contrary decreased; speed reduced or quickened. Some horses find it easiest to change at the end of a half pass. The advantages or disadvantages of any of those possibilities are revealed by the straightness or lack thereof of the canter.

Besides this, one cannot give more precise advice. Every trainer ought to have experience of the various methods and ought to be able to choose in each particular case the one most likely to produce the right result. The horse will be quick to show him whether he is correct or incorrect. One should not hesitate to abandon one method as soon as it seems that it is not leading to success. Dogged adhesion to one system shows poor horsemanship; what matters is the end result. In the case of especially difficult horses, one may even need to frequently reverse the usual order of movements; nevertheless, the basic principles of dressage need to be understood and respected—adaptability does not mean haphazard experimentation.

Whichever system one starts with, fine feeling and acute observation of the horse's reaction are essential; even so it is not easy to judge events accurately from the saddle. One really cannot dispense with the assistance of an expert who can see horse and rider as a whole and is able to give advice that can help one to improve one's aids.

If the rider is relatively inexperienced, it can be very helpful if possible to let him ride a horse so perfectly schooled in the flying changes that he does not need great expertise to obtain them. The teacher explains to the rider that he must do a half halt at a point immediately before the intended place for the flying change, then slide his outside leg forward to the girth at the same time as he changes the disposition of his weight; he must almost simultaneously press his new outside leg somewhat backwards to demand the flying change. As he changes his position, the rider must also change the flexion of the horse's head, without bending the neck in the direction of the new canter. Therefore, instead of pulling with the new inside rein, the rider must yield sufficiently with the previous outside rein to allow the change of flexion. All this must happen very quickly but smoothly (abruptness would upset the horse), in the course of the last stride of the canter before the change, thus allowing the horse to change legs during the subsequent period of suspension.

Sitting upright correctly, the rider must constantly correlate his own movements with those of the horse. In his first attempts at obtaining the change, as he concentrates on changing leg, rein and weight disposition, he may well forget that he must continue to drive the horse forward with inside seat bone and hip (Figure 41).

The outcome will vary depending on the idiosyncratic canter action and sensitivity of the horse. With horses that are inclined to rush or pull, it is unwise to let them gain speed and the point of change must be chosen with discernment (the best place is probably just before approaching a corner of the arena). On the contrary, with horses that tend to lag, one usually has to drive forward more emphatically and perhaps increase speed before the point of change.

If the horse lifts his croup it can be because he is not yet sufficiently master of his equilibrium, but it is often also because the rider displaces his outside leg too far back and hits with his heel the ticklish spot of the horse's flank, or because he pulls on the reins.

Swaying of the croup, amounting sometimes to just plain crookedness, is usually due to insufficient driving effect of the inside leg or to predominant use of the outside leg. If it occurs only to one side, it is probably because the natural one-sidedness of the horse has not yet been corrected. However, in successive changes at close intervals, what may look from behind like a disalignment of the croup (and is in reality a correct change of position), with correct bend the inside hind staying in line with the inside forefoot, cannot be described as swaying of the croup.

If the horse changes behind before changing in front or conversely, the rider or the horse can be at fault. In the first instance, either the half halt or the aids for change may be inadequate.

But it is not always the rider's fault. It can be that of the horse, for any number of reasons which cannot all be mentioned. For example, a basically faulty canter, with even only slightly delayed or hurried footfalls behind, nearly always produces an impure canter change. Some unknowledgeable spectators may be deceived, but not dressage experts and certainly not the other competitors carefully looking out for faults.

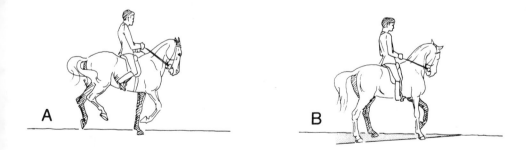

Figure 41: *Incorrect flying change:* **A** = *Lifting of the croup;* **B** = *Deviation with the hindquarters.*

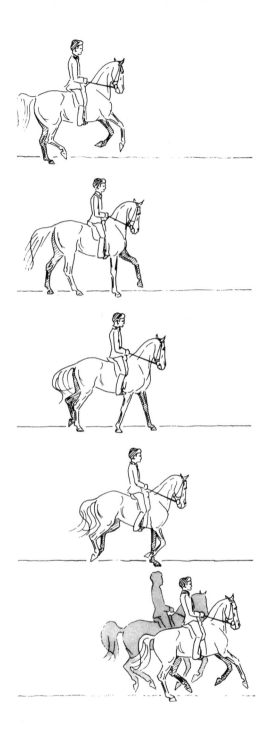

Figure 42: *Incorrect flying change; split change in left canter after the phase of suspension.*

In this case, it is first the canter itself that requires attention; the speed may need adjusting, the hindquarters may have to be either more or less loaded. If the horse changes in front before changing behind, one can canter in travers-like position before asking for the change. If on the contrary the horse changes behind first, a hint of shoulder-in position would be appropriate.

All the faults mentioned so far and some others may come to light when one starts to teach the flying change. What can one do when all known remedies fail? Even hard-boiled experts have had to acknowledge defeat in some cases. But, as Otto Digeon de Monteton said over a hundred years ago: "Until you have come to the end of your wits [in solving a problem with a particular horse], you cannot claim to be a horseman."

Furthermore, one recognizes genuine experts by their awareness and admission of their own difficulties. They appreciate the knowledge and the advice of their fellows. It is only the dilettante who boasts that he never has any problems and does not need help; he may not know it but it is unlikely that he will get very far.

Violence, as we know, is of no avail. It only serves to deepen the horse's aversion to the exercise to the extent that he openly rebels at the first indication of the rider's intention or puts up passive resistance, which is even worse.

The hindquarters of a horse that has not been taught to canter straight cannot be controlled by the rider's legs. Straightness at the canter is the first condition of correct execution of the changes. The horse must, of course, be capable of understanding the aids. In this respect one must always remember the maxim that applies to the whole process of schooling horses: *"It is not the duty of the horse to guess his rider's intention, but the duty of the rider to get himself understood by the horse."* The difference is important.

Next in importance to straightness are style and speed. A fluent flying change is inconceivable in the absence of impulsion.

The right degree of collection varies with the individual but, in any case, active elevation of head and neck, which stiffens the back, or over-bending (a fault often due to the use of draw reins), which causes overloading of the forehand, equally impairs the fluency of the change.

When one begins teaching the lesson, one must carefully observe to which side, at what place and at what speed the horse changes most easily. The place must be changed as soon as the horse reacts satisfactorily to the aids and also if he anticipates the indications of the rider. On the other hand, if he continually declines to change to one side, this will always be the "stiff" side, and clearly indicates marked one-sidedness and unequal contact which must be corrected before proceeding with the lesson.

The change of the rider's leg position should be moderate especially at the beginning as exaggerated leg movement surprises and annoys the horse. However, the effect of the outside leg can be reinforced by the spur (sometimes by two touches in rapid succession) or by the whip; on the other hand, what may be needed is more emphatic action of the new inside leg.

If all one's efforts remain unavailing, it may be that the horse has absolutely no aptitude for flying changes (which can only be decided after repeated attempts at intervals of some months) or that he is not ready for the lesson. This can be a question of age, of intelligence, or of deficient tractability. Horses do not all reach maturity at the same age. With sufficiently long experience of training horses for dressage, one will have met with some that despite excellent aptitudes, competent and carefully progressive training, have defeated so many endeavors to get them to execute a correct flying change as to make one seriously start to doubt their suitability for competition at a high level of proficiency. But after a fairly long, though "creative pause," all of a sudden they take to the exercise with every appearance of enjoyment.

They are like some gifted children who seem to be quite block-headed in their first years at school and all at once brighten up and surprise their teachers by their intelligence. Time can work wonders. It may seem that to have to wait three years before a horse is ready to compete at Third Level is excessive, but one should reflect that most have needed a much longer period of preparation. And after achieving the first correct isolated flying changes, the series of changes at every four, three or two strides, and eventually at every stride, are still very far away.

However, once correct isolated flying changes to both sides are well established and can be performed also from counter-canter to counter-canter, it is time to proceed with the changes after a given number of strides. No further explanation is necessary; the principles remain the same. It remains a matter of progressiveness and one should expect a few hitches. The flying changes at every stride are the crowning achievement, but there are horses which will always remain incapable of really mastering them.

Chapter 11

Canter Pirouette

The canter-pirouette has its origin in those far gone days when extreme maneuverability of the horse was required for man-to-man combat in war. In a somewhat different form it remains part of the repertoire of horses used in bull-fighting or cattle-roping.

Regardless of its practical advantages, in all systems of training and especially in the classical school, great importance has always been attached to the perfect execution of the canter-pirouette.

It is certainly one of the most difficult movements demanded of a horse. Some horses may have a certain natural aptitude for the piaffe, the passage or the flying change at every stride and will even perform them of their own accord once they feel secure in their equilibrium. But the canter-pirouette is a movement that no horse will ever execute spontaneously.

A pirouette in six to eight bounds of canter (which is what one should aim for) is the ultimate touchstone of collection, of flexibility of the haunches, of carrying power of the hindquarters, of impulsion, and of absolute submission to the aids. As Col. Podhajsky put it so well: "Piaffe and passage can be purchased ready made; the pirouette has to be ridden." This is the essential difference as far as dressage competitors who do not train their horses themselves are concerned.

As they must be performed to both hands and therefore twice in the advanced tests and because, unlike passage and piaffe, a coefficient of 2 is applied to them, canter-pirouettes have as decisive an influence on victory in modern friendly contests in a dressage arena as they once had on the battlefield.

Here is the definition of the pirouette (or half-pirouete) given by the FEI:

1. The pirouette (half-pirouette) is a circle (half circle) executed on two tracks, with a radius equal to the length of the horse, the forehand moving round the hindquarters.

2. Pirouettes (half-pirouettes) are usually carried out at collected walk or canter, but can also be executed at piaffe.

3. At the pirouette (half-pirouette) the forefeet and the outside hind foot move round the inside hind foot, which is at the center of the circle and should return to the same spot or rather very slightly in front of it, each time it leaves the ground.

4. At whatever gait the pirouettes (half-pirouettes) are executed,

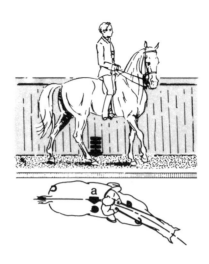

Figure 43: *Right shoulder-in at canter;* a = *Engagement of inside hind foot.*

the horse slightly bent in the direction in which he is turning, should remain "on the bit" with a light contact, and turn smoothly, maintaining exactly the same rhythm and sequence of footfalls characteristic of that gait.

5. During the pirouettes (half-pirouettes) the horse should maintain impulsion and never in the slightest way move backwards or deviate sideways. If the inside hind foot is not raised and returned to the ground in the same rhythm as the outside hind foot, the gait is no longer regular.

The first paragraph clearly describes the movement.

Since the smaller the radius of a volte on two tracks the more difficult it is to maintain the regularity of the gait, it follows that a movement on a circle of a radius not exceeding the length of the horse is very difficult indeed. It also follows that the canter-pirouette must be prepared by the practice of voltes on two tracks of progressively reduced diameter.

It is to the execution of this work that we will first devote our attention.

Some time ago a rider confidentially told me that his horse had mastered all that was required in advanced tests, except the confounded pirouette. It seemed to me that if the pirouette was impossible, something else was amiss. It turned out that the horse could not fluently execute a half-pirouette at the walk, and he could not canter on a 6 m volte without turning out his hindquarters and altering

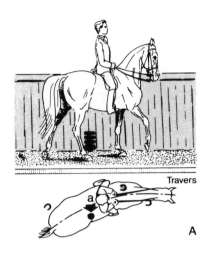

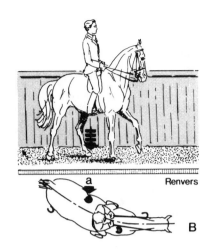

Figure 44: **A** = *Travers in right canter;* **B** = *Renvers in left canter.* **a** = *Engagement of inside hind.*

the rhythm of the canter, and that he could not even turn the corners of the arena at a collected canter without difficulty. Considering those circumstances, a volte on two tracks of any diameter would be impossible. The canter pirouette is fairly included in advance dressage tests and any difficulty a horse may experience in executing it must be attributed to negligence on the part of the trainer. However talented a horse may be, sooner or later one must suffer the consequences of impatience or laziness and skipping of the tedious ironing out of imperfections.

No horse can be expected to canter on two tracks on small voltes before he has become absolutely proficient in the lateral movements in canter on straight lines, and then on large circles. Whether and when the diameter of the circle can be reduced depends on the progress of the horse. If the canter becomes sluggish or impure or if he breaks to trot on the tighter circle, one must conclude that he is still not ready for the more difficult exercise (Figures 44 and 45).

The work starts with shoulder-in and travers along the wall and leads through the half pass to reduction and enlargement of the circle. This exercise, carried out alternately to one hand and the other, strengthens both hind limbs, and the inside one especially during the enlargement of the circle. It is weakness of the inside hind that causes the horse to stiffen the haunches in the turns and, of course, a correct canter pirouette is inconceivable if the horse resists flexion of all the joints of that limb (reducing and enlarging the circle is an extremely

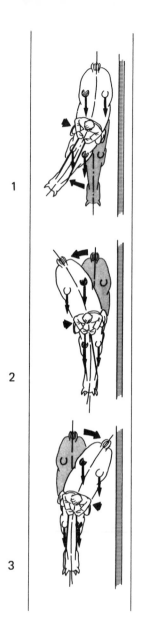

Figure 45: *Lateral movement at canter. Comparison of position of the horse in movement on one or on two tracks.* **1** = *Right shoulder-in;* **2** = *Right travers;* **3** = *Left renvers.*

important exercise in the preparation of the pirouette). The subsequent reduction of the diameter of the circles, and then of the voltes on two tracks, is a procedure that has never failed to produce excellent results when the exercise is progressively practiced.

To facilitate control of the hindquarters, at the beginning it is advisable to "square" the voltes by using the corners of the arena and to start with a square volte of a diameter of 10 m. On this 10 m square volte one canters in a slight renvers position, not exceeding a distance of one or two hoof widths between the two tracks since the most important thing is maintenance of an even speed. Renvers is more suitable than travers for two reasons. First, because it is more difficult to control the hindquarters in the latter position. Secondly, because in renvers, as the hind feet are placed on the outside track they have to travel farther and, in addition, (providing he uses his outside leg effectively) in the corners the rider is in a better position to teach the horse to engage his hindquarters obediently in the direction of the forehand (Figure 46).

However, as soon as the horse can execute the volte in renvers fluently, without deterioration of collection one can change to travers, perhaps with less bend, which can be done without changing direction. Little by little the square volte in travers can be made smaller and rounder until it becomes a true volte on two tracks.

Some may question the advisability of starting with a square volte. It is advisable because not only does the square volte, as has already been said, enable better control, but also because each turning of a corner amounts to a quarter of a pirouette (Figure 47).

Since all that has been said about the pirouette applies, of course, also to the half-pirouette, one can start by riding demi-voltes instead of complete voltes.

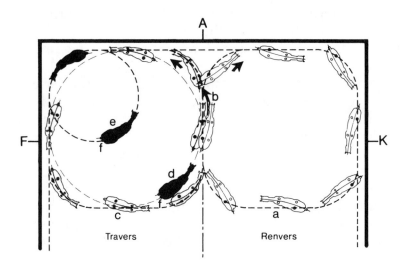

Figure 46: *The square volte.* **a** = *Canter in renvers;* **b** = *Changing to travers;* **c, d,** **e** = *Rounding off the corner and progressively diminishing the dimension of the volte on two tracks to 6 m.;* **f** = *6 m. volte on one track.*

Many variations of this sort of exercise depending on the particular aptitudes of the horse will suggest themselves to the adaptable and thinking trainer who is prepared to take enough trouble. For example, a demi-volte on two tracks can be executed on the centerline after a half pass, to return to the wall in half pass, and then do a flying change and repeat the exercise to the other hand. It is easy to verify whether the demi-volte ends on the centerline.

Conscientious progressiveness in decreasing the radius of the volte on two tracks eventually leads to the pirouette, which is not just a turn, but the smallest possible volte on two tracks possible to execute at a regular canter.

Trying to do a canter pirouette without having gone through this fairly lengthy preparation is as absurd as attempting to make an insufficiently trained horse jump a two-meter high obstacle in a Puissance competition. In show-jumping, however, one can hear the rapping of the wall, if the horse has not had the sense to run out or to stop. In a badly executed pirouette, on the other hand, an uninformed spectator may not detect anything amiss unless his hearing is good enough to perceive the grinding sound made by bone moving upon bone in the abused hind joints. The noise is not as loud and the consequences are less dramatic; nevertheless it shows equally bad horsemanship. Pulling a horse or throwing him around to turn him on the spot can in no way be described as executing a canter pirouette which is supposed to be graceful movement.

In a correctly executed pirouette, the horse continues to canter; the maintenance of the canter is the most important thing. If the hind feet stick to the ground while the forehand revolves, the turn is not a pirouette.

Those sort of turns on the spot are inevitable if the horse has not been carefully prepared. Out of habit, horses may well obey the turning aids, but they do not understand what in reality they are supposed to do. To continue cantering while turning absolutely on the spot is in any case impossible; the flexion of the hocks in a correct canter pirouette is strenuous enough. Some forward movement must always be allowed. Even in the half-pirouette at walk or piaffe, the horse has to step forward, be it by only a few centimeters. In the canter pirouette it is for the maintenance of the canter that the rider must strive, and the hind feet must be allowed to move on a slightly larger circle than at walk or piaffe.

The aids for the canter pirouette are the same as for the turn on the haunches or the walk pirouette and it is unnecessary to say more about them here. The only difference is that they must be combined with the aids for canter.

The canter strides must already be shortened before reaching the prescribed place for the pirouette to avoid the risk of spoiling the rhythm by shortening them at the moment of starting the turn. Then a clear half halt is given with the outside rein, and the horse must

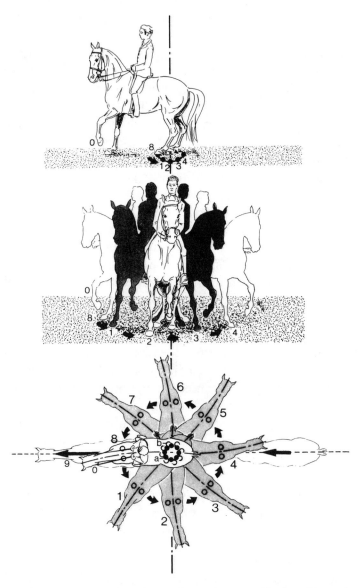

Figure 47: *Canter pirouette.* **O** = *Start of turn (same as 8);* **9** = *Cantering straight ahead after completion of the pirouette.* **a** = *Inside hind foot (main support);* **b** = *Outside hind foot.*

continue to canter on a very small circle and complete the pirouette in six to eight strides. No more steps should be made with the forefeet than the hind ones. Each bound of the canter is determined by the rider's outside rein and inside leg. The outside leg prevents a turning out of the hindquarters or any attempt the horse may make to throw himself into the turn of his own initiative or to continue turning after the pirouette is completed. At any moment during the movement, one should be able to stop the turn and continue to canter on a straight line (Figure 47).

The rider's seat is of utmost importance. He should not lean backward or forward and must drive the horse powerfully forward with his seat bones, especially the inside one, at each bound of the canter. Since the legs must be used as aids for the turn and the hands cannot have any effect on the maintenance of the gait, it is only the driving effect of the seat that can sustain the canter. The horse will cease to canter the moment the rider ceases to use his seat with suppleness and sufficient vigor. As soon as the pirouette is completed, a half halt with the outside rein and, almost simultaneously, the pressure of both legs and the driving action of the seat send the horse forward on the straight line with a reduced degree of collection at the normal speed of collected canter. The flying change shortly after the pirouette required in advanced international tests would be bungled if the rider failed to obtain sufficient forward movement in the limited space available.

It is when the movement is wrongly executed as an about-turn on the spot that the subsequent canter on the straight is likely to deteriorate. The horse may break the canter, and this would be just as deplorable as if he had executed a volte at walk instead of canter. Therefore, within limits of course, judges should not mark as severely a little too much forward movement in the pirouette as a disruption of the canter. The latter is usually due to insufficient preparation by work on voltes on two tracks or by the rider leaning back and overloading the hindquarters. Trying to compensate for this by elevating the forehand by strength of arms merely heightens the bad impression made on judges and knowledgeable spectators.

Turning too slowly is just as bad as throwing the forehand round hurriedly. If the horse is not yet sufficiently capable of collecting himself on a small enough circle to be called a pirouette, it is better to put up with too big a volte than to provoke and tolerate an irregular rhythm in the gait.

The correct distribution of weight must always remain a major concern. In classical equitation even the turn on the forehand requires a certain measure of collection and self-carriage since its purpose is to get the horse to engage and start flexing his hocks. One should remember, however, that active, and excessive elevation of the neck does not lighten the forehand. It has the reverse effect; it causes a hollowing and stiffening of the back which prevents engagement of the hindquarters.

When a horse's hind limbs lack strength and resilience, he obeys the turning aids but is incapable of springing off his haunches in collected canter.

In the pirouette one must therefore avoid using mostly the reins to make the horse turn. The main turning aids must reside in the legs and seat. But one must also beware of braking too much with the reins to enforce a pirouette absolutely on the spot. Trying to gather the horse with force of arms causes the hind feet to stick to the ground and the horse either to lean on the hand or simply let his hind limbs drag behind.

In the pirouette the rider's hand must allow with each stride the spring in the canter. A correctly collected horse will not attempt to run away and, as in the piaffe, a light contact results in a much more fluent movement than a taut rein.

Exaggerated lateral weight effect compromises the horse's equilibrium as much as does exaggerated leaning backward. It only shows that the rider is trying to compensate for lack of adequate schooling by the use of forcible aids.

One must remember that as the pirouette is a travers sort of turn on the haunches it necessitates optimum overall bend so that the hindquarters can be held ever so slightly inward during the whole execution of the movement. Otherwise the hindquarters are liable to turn out at the end of the turn or the horse may change lead.

But the horse must not canter on two tracks in the approach and the very slight travers position must not be apparent before the beginning of the pirouette. Preserving the straightness of the canter before and after the pirouette is an additional difficulty.

During schooling, and especially re-schooling, the pirouette naturally can be combined with the half pass. Since the horse is then already moving on two tracks, it is easier to preserve the bend during the pirouettes. Finishing the pirouette with a half pass also helps to make the horse understand he must not throw out his hindquarters at the end of the turn.

On the other hand, it is sometimes the inside hind that hinders the pirouette by deviating towards the inside in order to avoid having to support the weight and flex the haunch. The evasion is prevented by putting the horse in a slight shoulder-in position just before the turn and driving particularly emphatically with the inside leg during the first and the subsequent bounds of the canter pirouette. At the end of the pirouette one continues to canter in the same shoulder-in position for a short distance.

When the preparatory work described above has produced the intended result, it is time to enhance the difficulty of the pirouette. First, one does one or two "test" bounds of canter to verify that the horse is capable of sustaining the gait more or less on the spot on two tracks and can be turned easily. Then, after a half halt, the forehand is directed towards the middle of the short side of the arena by having the horse turn on the haunches; no more than two strides of the canter are called for and they must feel perfectly easy. One continues the canter on the centerline, where the exercise can perhaps be repeated to the same hand.

The next stage is the half-pirouette in three or four springs. It can be very useful to ask for it on some part of a circle and, if collection and bend are found to be not quite sufficient, one or two voltes can be executed at the chosen place to improve them before trying the half-pirouette. It is always advisable to try the first half-pirouette on the "closed" side of the circle. After completion of the turning movement, one continues in counter-canter on the circle to execute the second half-pirouette on the "open side," thus returning to true canter. It should also be noted that many horses find it easier in the beginning to execute a half-pirouette after a half pass to the middle of the centerline and then to half pass back to the original line instead of having to perform the movement on a straight line as is required in the Prix St. Georges.

With particularly forward-going horses, half passing on the diagonal of the half-school and executing the half-pirouette at a distance of a horse's length from the wall is a practical way of taking advantage of the restraining influence of the latter.

From the half-pirouette one proceeds to the three-quarter pirouette. One canters in renvers towards the far corner on the second track parallel to the long side, lightens the forehand with a half halt before executing a three-quarter pirouette outwards, continues in renvers on the second track of the short side to execute another three-quarter pirouette at the next corner, and so on. However, the rider must always remain conscious of the fact that for the horse the pirouette is one of the most strenuous of dressage movements and that fatigue is frequently the cause of flawed execution. The advantages of the above exercise is that the renvers on the second track makes it easy for the rider to control direction and bend by constantly maintaining the same distance from the wall, and that the risk of turning more than one intends is avoided.

The full pirouette at the point of change of hand on the diagonal and finally on the centerline is the crowning achievement, but should not now present any difficulty with proper preparation. At the end of the second half of the small circle described by the hind feet the pirouette, if all goes, well should be completed where it started.

Some thoroughly prepared and very talented horses find the pirouette so easy that they may repeat it of their own accord several times giving thus an impressive demonstration of agility and tractability. But this should not be overdone; disparagers of dressage are only too ready to say that it is "show-business" and that the advanced movements are just circus acts.

Chapter 12

The Rein Back and the *Schaukel*

A rein back that absolutely conforms to the rules of classical equitation is a very difficult movement. This statement may surprise those who are happy to continue competing at the lower level of the discipline, but its truth is averred by all horsemen dedicated to the higher education of horses. The subject is therefore worth discussion in some depth.

We should bear in mind to start with that backward stepping is not a movement natural to horses. We must also clearly understand the point of teaching them not just to rein back but to do so in a manner conforming to the rules of classical equitation.

One must, of course, distinguish between the use of the rein back for practical purposes and for the purpose of High School dressage. There are situations in which the horse's understanding of this requirement is essential and all riding horses must be taught to obey without fuss the aids for the rein back.

In the first case all that is necessary is that the horse step backwards in diagonals willingly, calmly, and regularly at the bidding of the rider while remaining straight and on the bit.

In higher levels of dressage, however, the rein back loses its utilitarian value and becomes an exercise intended to improve collection by loading the hindquarters and increasing the flexion of the haunches. Instead of being an end in itself, it is a means to an end.

Collection can only be increased if it already exists. Therefore, it is always necessary to gather the horse by executing a transition halt before demanding a step of the rein back. Satisfactory performance of the transition must be considered in detail also, but it will be done later.

What should a correct classical rein back look like? First, the horse must have been strongly collected by the correct transition to halt, to the effect of placing the hind feet exactly under the horse's hip joints. He must then move backwards perfectly straight, in short, regular, diagonal steps at about the speed of the collected walk, with croup lowered, hind limbs loaded, and their joints well flexed. The horse must not drag his hind feet; they have to be distinctly lifted. His neck must be arched and elevated, the poll flexed to put the nose slightly ahead of the ventrical, and he must chew the bit softly without opening his mouth. He must not make one step more or less than commanded by the aids. If one wishes to stop the movement by means of another halt, the horse must calmly allow himself to be slightly more gathered (Figure 48).

This is the ideal rein back. It supposes a horse that is perfectly calm and has been carefully schooled so that he has ceased to oppose any resistance to collection either by the mouth, the poll or the hind joints.

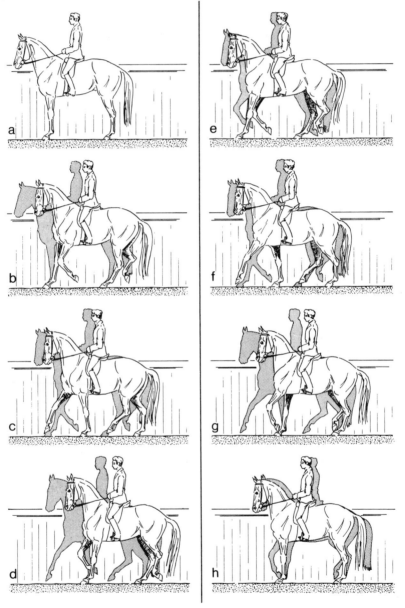

Figure 48: *The rein back.* **a-f** = *Correct sequence of movements in each stride of the rein back;* **g, h** = *The halt at the end of the rein back.*

But what are the mechanics of the movement? Do the backward stepping hind limbs pull the forelimbs back with them? Or do the forelimbs push the hind limbs backwards? Why is the movement such an unnatural one for the horse? What are the aids for the rein back? All those questions have to be answered.

In some manner or another even a relatively untrained horse will step backwards on demand, but the manner will usually differ very much from the one required in classical equitation. The manner of execution of the movement depends on the distribution of weight between forehand and hindquarters, on the degree of straightness in movement, and on the submissiveness and flexibility of haunches and poll. For utilitarian purposes, it does not matter if the body is pushed backwards by the backward-stepping forelimbs. In dressage, wherein the rein back is used to improve the flexion of haunches already obtained by the various collecting exercises previously described, it is the hindquarters that take the forehand back. The flexion of the haunches lightens and elevates the forehand. Therefore, the forefeet must be lifted higher than the loaded hind feet. This can result, depending on weight distribution, in a disruption of simultaneity of the diagonal steps hardly perceptible to the human eye, which is of no importance if it is not obvious and if there is no deviation from a straight line. It would be too punctilious and quite wrong to deduct even one mark on this account if the rein back is in other ways correct. As one highly reputed judge often used to say, "it is impossible, thank heavens, to measure the movements of a horse in millimeters and grams." We should not forget that in a perfectly diagonal trot each hind limb in turn projects the body forward and upwards, but that in the rein back the weight of the heavy limb has to be lifted against inertia. Far less effort is required to straighten the limb than to lift it up.

The rein back can justifiably be said to be an unnatural movement because it is contrary to the natural instinct and the normal mechanics of movement of horses. By reason of bodily structure and mental make-up, a well-bred horse has a strong propensity for forward movement; his atavistic escape reflex has not been eradicated by centuries of domestication. It is only rarely that one can observe a horse at liberty stepping backwards. If he does so, it is never by more than one or two steps, and even then he avoids loading his hindquarters by displacing his croup more or less sideways. The anatomical leverage system of his hind limbs is designed to propel the animal forward with economy of effort and to facilitate quick acceleration. It is not so well suited to rearward movement. As a result, the steps in a classically correct rein back must always be shorter than the steps of a collected walk.

We now consider the aids and effects that determine the rein back. Once again one is reminded that there are various ways of executing all movements depending on the stage of schooling and the degree of education of the horse and whether the lesson serves a purely practical purpose or the ends of advanced dressage. The correct transition to halt is a good example. With a novice horse one would expect him to be able to come to a square halt with his weight equally distributed over all four limbs, but it would be wrong to demand greater engagement of the hind feet than that or to expect the horse to remain perfectly on the bit for any length of time. On the other hand, in the most advanced tests the dressage horse is required to stand completely motionless for a certain period of time, with hind feet equally engaged under his hips, hindquarters more loaded than the forehand, haunches flexed, nose almost perpendicular to the ground, neck elevated, on a light contact while chewing the bit calmly and regularly. This sort of halt can be executed and demanded only if the horse has been rationally schooled up to a point where his education can be considered to be almost complete.

In between novice and advanced stages, there are many degrees of submission depending on the stage of schooling of the horse and the competence of the rider. The same applies to the rein back as to the halt and this explains the confusingly contradictory advice given by different text books and teachers which cause the bewildered student of horsemanship to wail: "What am I supposed to do? One teacher tells

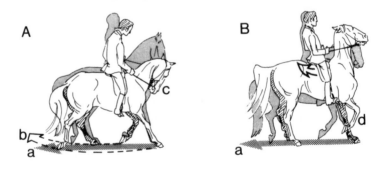

Figure 49: *Faulty rein back.* **a** = *Straight rein back.* **b** = *Lateral deviation of hindquarters;* **c** = *Horse pulled backwards by the reins, overbent and on the forehand;* **d** = *Above the bit, hollowed back, hind feet rooted to the ground.*

130

me to lean forward and lighten the horse's hindquarters, another tells me to sit deep and upright or even to lean backwards. One day I am told to use the hands alternately, another to use both reins simultaneously."

The pupil is right—but so is the teacher. In the case of a young or partly trained horse, one can be delighted if he consents to step backwards at all. A slight forward inclination of the rider's torso helps the backward movement of the horse. The reins are used alternately to turn the horse's head to one side then the other in order to prevent too much lateral displacement of the hindquarters, with the restraining hand effect being supplemented by the leg aid on the same side.

On the other hand, the classical rein back from the halt calls for a completely different procedure. First, it should be possible to maintain the collected horse at the halt for an appreciable moment, thus proving his perfect acceptance of the increased loading of the hindquarters. The halt may even have to be executed directly from a collected trot full of impulsion if the horse is disinclined to engage his hind feet sufficiently under the mass. Then the rider's leg must produce the impulsion that causes the horse to lift a hind foot. As soon as the motion is felt, both hands together must transform the incipient forward movement into a backward one. In fact, it should be possible to rein back while holding all the reins in one hand. The rider must load the hindquarters with his weight; his position must be perpendicular to the horse's back but, since the croup is lowered, this gives the appearance of a slight backward inclination of his trunk.

A rein back executed in this manner entails considerable flexion of the hind joints, especially of the hip and stifle, and is therefore a most suitable preparation for passage and piaffe. In recent Grand Prix tests it has been prescribed that the horse coming from A on the centerline at L halts, rein backs four steps and immediately proceeds at the passage. It can be observed that the passage shows considerably more expression after the rein back than before. Furthermore, those transitions demonstrate that modern advanced dressage has not—as is often falsely asserted—lost all resemblance to classical artistic horsemanship.

Considering that the rein back is on the one hand an excellent preparation for piaffe and passage, and on the other hand so difficult for the horse and contrary to his natural movement, one has to be careful to choose a method of teaching the movement which does not provoke understandable resistance.

What can the rider do if the horse completely ignores the aids and locks all his joints? The cause may reside just as likely in the forehand as the hindquarters. If the hind feet are not sufficiently engaged, the hocks being left behind, it is of course almost impossible for the horse to step backwards. It is equally impossible to obtain a step of the rein back if the horse stiffens the poll, the neck and the jaw. In such cases it is useless to continue attempting the movement before the horse has been made sufficiently submissive by other exercises, especially in the transition to the halt.

An even more unpleasant form of resistance is shown by a horse that refuses to obey the collecting aids and runs backwards hurriedly as soon as he feels the slightest opposition of the hand (Figure 49).

In this case, if the horse refuses to obey the forward driving effect of legs (supported perhaps by assistance from a person on the ground), one should first attempt to quietly rein back. If the horse continues to run backwards for some time, then get him to halt on the bit before finally allowing him to move forward and getting him to submit quietly to the aids of legs or hands. A few steps of rein back followed by a halt on the bit can then be again attempted.

It is a dangerous and wrong policy to abandon the contact as soon as the horse starts to run backwards, for it is precisely to achieve this result that he resorts to the maneuver. The antics would start all over again every time he was asked to rein back.

Long, hurried backward steps show resistance to collection and loading of hindquarters. Hesitance, on the contrary, betrays insufficient submissiveness. Sideways deviation of the croup should be corrected by the hand as well as the leg on the same side, rather than by the leg alone and one can also practice the movement along the wall.

If one realizes the difficulty of the rein back, one can easily imagine the trickiness of the *Schaukel*, combining as it does the difficult backward movement with the equally difficult collected walk. This is especially true as a specified number of steps must be executed flowing in one direction and then the other without a pause, and when the exercise is immediately repeated. The horse cannot be allowed to stop moving by letting one hind foot come to rest beside the opposite one. Perfect execution requires the highest degree of collection.

If one allowed the slightest lessening of collection in the walk, the smooth transition to rein back without a pause would be practically impossible. Conversely, if the horse lost some collection during the rein back, the ensuing stride of the gait that must succeed the last backward step would not be correct. It is possible that at some time a transition to extended walk out of the rein back will be demanded, which would be a considerable test of the rider's ability to preserve the horse's calm submission to the aids despite the high degree of collection required;

otherwise he would neither lengthen his frame to maintain the contact nor lengthen his stride sufficiently and would probably show some impure strides of the walk.

Carriage, elevation of head and neck, flexion of the poll, and chewing of the bit should all remain unaltered during the entire movement which must proceed on a perfectly straight line, with perfect regularity, on a light contact and in a high degree of collection. One cannot expect all horses, regardless of preparation, to be able to perform a perfect *Schaukel*. Nevertheless, those are the criteria of excellence.

The movement is the most revealing touchstone of perfect straightness and total submission to both the driving and restraining aids. In fact, there are very few horses, even among those who are very proficient in passage, piaffe, flying changes or pirouettes capable of executing a completely flawless *Schaukel*. It is therefore meat and drink for judges, especially the side ones; nothing else is as easy to find fault with.

In all the other lessons we have studied, impulsion is an important consideration and a horse's inclination to go forwards is a rider's greatest asset. But how can the criterion of impulsion be applied to the rein back which is the opposite of forward movement (or to complete immobility at the halt at the beginning of the test), or even to the collected walk? Those movements are, however, tests of perfect tractability and there are a number of horses that can do passage, piaffe, pirouettes and flying changes at every stride and yet are by no means absolutely tractable.

As for the *Schaukel* it is the supreme test of suppleness and submission of a horse and, since the judges have plenty of time to scrutinize every step of the movement, it amounts to a merciless exposure of any weakness in those respects.

In fact, it is such a severe test that one may wonder why it is not required in the Grand Prix Special whenever it is part of the Grand Prix, and why a coefficient is not applied. As in principle the Special must include some extra difficulty, one could perhaps demand that it not be dismissed as just another trick devised to make a rider's sufficiently difficult life more difficult still.

One could also possible combine the *Schaukel* with the half-pirouette and thus test a horse's submission to the lateral aids as well.

At our training establishment we have sometimes practiced what we call the "*Combi-Schaukel*" in the following form: five backward steps, four forward steps, three backward steps, four forward ones, five backward ones, and a pirouette to the left followed by extended walk.

I will not say more on this subject for fear of being suspected of having schaukelt (!) off my rocker!

Chapter 13

Piaffe and Passage

Both movements will be discussed in the same chapter, even though the connection is not as strong as it appears at first sight. A correct piaffe, with pronouncedly flexed haunches and extreme elevation of the forehand, is a test of the carrying capacity of the hindquarters combined with properly understood impulsion, which must not of course be confused with speed and gait.

The ratio of carrying capacity to impulsion and vice versa determines a horse's greater aptitude for the piaffe or for the passage. Through no fault of the rider, it is sometimes impossible to obtain a well-cadenced piaffe from a horse that excels at the passage, and the reverse also happens.

This goes to show that piaffe and passage are not so very closely related, so that one should not assume that if a horse can do the passage, he should be capable of doing piaffe just as well.

Furthermore, even when one can be quite satisfied with the execution of both of those movements, the transition from one to another may continue to remain a headache for months or years. It is perhaps only once in every ten years that one sees a horse that has perfectly mastered a fluent transition from a really graceful piaffe to an impressive passage and conversely.

Why the difficulty? Is it really inordinately difficult to teach horses to do either movement? The answer is no, provided of course that the horse has the required aptitudes. Consider the fiery Andalusians, for example, with their naturally well-angled hindquarters, their high action and lofty carriage, all combined with spirit and impulsion, and their relatives, the Lipizzaner of the Spanish Riding School of Vienna.

But in the modern sport of dressage, a different type of horse is preferred, one that has impressive, i.e. ground covering, basic gaits and is capable of "devouring" the ground with each stride of medium or extended trot on the line of the diagonal. This is a matter of conformation and mechanics of movement as much as of impulsion; and it is precisely this ability that makes it extremely difficult for them to lift their forefeet off the ground to the same extent as the type of horse favored in the XVIIIth century, of which the Lipizzaner and Lusitanos are good examples.

The converse is equally true and it is unreasonable to expect from the latter type the same aptitude for extended gaits as they possess for the elevated ones. Unfortunately, it seems that in international competitions there are few judges who are willing to take those factors into account.

Still there is, thank heavens, sufficient variety in the equine world of our time and there is as much enjoyment to be found in riding one type or the other. It may be that all horses will conform to a uniform standard in the future, and then dressage will have lost much of its appeal.

The masters of horsemanship of past centuries gave extremely detailed recipes for training horses in both of the movements. However, for the reason just explained, we cannot hope to emulate them. So much has been written on the subject by modern experts that it sometimes seems that nothing more needs to be said.

But although their bookshelves may already be crammed with the works of authors of all times, specialists in any subject cannot resist adding to their collection and carefully study every new publication devoted to their particular interest. It is not always in the hope of discovering something entirely new, but because they like to compare the experience of other experts with their own. A slightly different approach to a difficulty (small cause, great effects) may help them to find the answer to a particular problem. In all sciences—and horsemanship is a science as much as an art—experts know that they can learn a lot from one another.

For example, we find that generally it is recommended that the passage should not be taught before a horse has learned the piaffe. Briefly, the reasons are that: 1) a better passage is obtained; 2) there is a risk of the collected trot becoming too cadenced or hovering when the horse learns the passage before the piaffe; and 3) many horses become tense in the first stages of learning to passage before they can do the piaffe and it may take a long time to get them to unwind. The piaffe, on the other hand, is extremely favorable to the improvement of the collected trot.

Yet some authorities say that there are cases when it can be a great advantage to teach the passage first. For example, when a horse tends to "run" at the collected trot, teaching him to passage is one way of obtaining more cadence in the trot. However, those cases are rather exceptional.

There is a logical progression in the tests devised by the FEI, even though they may be criticized on points of detail. For instance, it is right that only the piaffe be required in the Intermediate II and that some forward movement is to be seen. This is to discourage riders from demanding too early a piaffe absolutely on the spot, with serious adverse consequences which will be discussed further on.

It is also logical to include the passage for the first time in the Grand Prix, and to demand that the first passage be developed from the collected walk which is sufficient proof of correctness of the latter gait, so essential to the preparation of the former.

There are so-called dressage horses that spontaneously go into a sort of passage, which may fool uninformed spectators but would shame a knowledgeable dressage rider, and are encouraged to do so by their impatient riders even before they can trot correctly. By demanding the transition to passage from the collected walk, any omissions in the education of the horse are clearly revealed.

The successful dressage rider does not stray from the difficult path that leads from novice to Grand Prix. He does not allow his horse to present him with flying changes before he can counter-canter. Neither does he let the horse produce passage-like steps while he is still trying to get him to trot collectedly with sufficient energy and regularity to satisfy the requirements of the important elementary and medium tests. This rider's motto is "all in good time." The ambitious but impatient rider is happy to accept whatever his horse offers, is quite unconcerned by any shortcomings and glories in the talent of his half-educated animal. But, of course, it takes inordinate dedication to work hard at a discipline in which every step, every line, even the slightest unwanted movement (like head nodding or tail swishing at the halt) matters and this is not to every rider's liking. It demands a huge amount of self-control.

It is logical to teach the piaffe before the passage. A detailed description of these movements is beyond the scope of the present work and there is no point in repeating all that has so often been said and written elsewhere. I will just explain some procedures that can usefully be employed, the faults to avoid, and the means available to the rider to correct the faults that may creep in.

If the horse is particularly talented, the piaffe may be taught directly from the saddle without recourse to the assistance of a person on the ground and work in hand. On the whole, however, it is easier to get the horse to understand the new strange requirement when he is unburdened by the weight of the rider.

Work In Hand

Work in hand always makes it easier for the horse to learn to do the piaffe and, when the results are entirely satisfactory, significant difficulty in obtaining the movement from the saddle is unlikely. There are, however, some riders who appear to have a very wrong conception of work in hand, especially in the later stages when the horse's execution of the movement approaches perfection. They seem to think that they need only stand quietly beside the horse, restraining him very lightly in front while encouraging him a little from behind—child-like play really, that anybody can imitate. It is true that it should look so easy but appearances are deceptive. In fact, with a horse that has mastered a really good piaffe, it is more beneficial, although it takes much more skill, to get him to advance imperceptibly during the execution of the movement instead of moving his limbs without gaining a fraction of ground.

In any case, to avoid resistance and conflict, one should beware of starting work in hand too early. Side reins must be adjusted to a length suitable for a collected trot. The horse must, therefore, be prepared to be gathered at least to the degree expected in medium tests.

The side reins may be attached either to the saddle or the surcingle. A cavesson, besides the double or single bridle, must be used, with a fairly short leading rein buckled to the middle ring. The "tapper" (a kind of rod about 2 m long) is held in the right hand. We call it a tapper rather than a whip, because its function is not to chase or tickle but merely to administer light touches to the horse's body. It is designed for work in hand and cannot be replaced by a broken lunging whip, for example. It must be long enough to allow precision in its use and a measure of safety, and must therefore be light. The shaft should taper from a thickness at one end which enables one to hold it easily to a fairly pointed extremity.

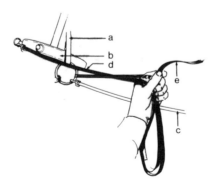

Figure 50: *Equipment for work in hand.* **a** = *Cheek piece of snaffle;* **b** = *Nose band of cavesson;* **c** = *Side rein;* **d** = *Lead rein;* **e** = *Snaffle rein secured behind pulled up stirrup.*

The cavesson also needs to be of the correct kind; it must have a well padded nose band without a central link. It must fit perfectly. The only moveable part should be the middle ring.

Side reins with an elastic inset are not suitable because they do not give sufficiently precise control. In fact, they encourage the horse to push against the bit (Figure 51).

A spring hook is affixed to one end of the lead rein which has a loop at the other end. This need not be used in the later stages of the work when the horse can be trusted to accept without protest the restraint imposed by the short reins and can keep the appropriate position of his own accord for a sufficiently long period of time.

The horse must, of course, be introduced very cautiously to the tapper. He certainly must respect, but not fear it. Work in hand is extremely dangerous or quite impossible when a horse panics at the mere sight of the tapper. He may rear, lash out violently or bolt.

Distrust and fear always have catastrophic consequences. The recalcitrant horse becomes almost impossible to control and his resistance can suddenly turn into blind fury.

In the beginning, one should beware especially of an unexpected defensive reaction inspired by the horse's apprehension of danger as the trainer gets closer. Riders who have not regularly handled and groomed horses cannot know how quickly a horse that feels he cannot escape an imaginary danger can be gripped by a powerful instinct to defend himself violently. They may be too slow to notice warning signs and to get out of the way of the furious animal's terrible weapons. It would be extremely foolhardy for such riders to experiment with work in hand.

Figure 51: *Suitable points of application of the tapper.* **a** = *On the croup in the region of the hip bone;* **b** = *In the region of the buttocks;* **c** = *In the region of the stifle.*

To gain the horse's trust, one must first start to accustom him to the tapper by gently stroking it all over his body and at the end of the lesson patting him on the neck with the other hand or perhaps offering a delicacy. The horse is placed preferably with his right side against the long side of the arena. When he is completely calm and yet attentive, he can be persuaded to move forwards by touches of the tapper on the rib cage close to the girth or on the hind limb (Figure 52).

One should not try to obtain piaffe-like steps at the beginning of the work by totally preventing forward movement with the lead rein while demanding it with the tapper. The horse would become very confused and would almost certainly lash out more or less violently behind. Instead, one should aim at producing an active but very collected trot, with steps so short that one need not run backwards to go with the forward movement. The horse cannot be deemed ready for work in hand if this result is unobtainable. His previous education should have produced a degree of submission such that the trot can be shortened sufficiently by the opposition of the cavesson (reinforced if necessary by the left snaffle rein) to the forward movement without declining to the walk.

The horse must consent to flex at the poll, and if the suppleness of this region is not yet sufficient, work in hand must be postponed until flexibility has been developed by logical daily schooling under saddle.

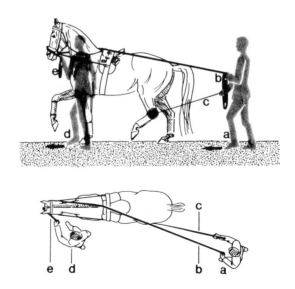

Figure 52: *The work in hand with an assistant.* **a** = *Trainer follows the horse;* **b** = *The lunge;* **c** = *Tapper;* **d** = *Assistant guides the horse;* **e** = *Lead rein*

In many cases, two persons are needed to carry out the work. An assistant guides the horse by his head while the trainer holds the lunge and carefully urges the horse forward with the tapper while walking behind him and slightly to his left at a safe enough distance. The lunge is attached to the right snaffle ring and passes over the saddle to the trainer's hand. The role of the assistant is not to restrain by force and both hands a horse that is as yet unable to flex all his joints adequately. He is there merely to direct the horse on the track at a sufficient distance from the wall and to regulate the speed until the horse understands the new requirement. The assistant must implicitly obey the instructions of the trainer and it is desirable that he himself have some knowledge, experience and feeling. The help of assistant can be dispensed with as soon as the horse is ready to start the piaffe.

However, if possible, it is easier for the trainer to carry out the work alone. He can see only to a limited extent and certainly cannot feel how much the assistant has on his hands. When the trainer can hold rein and tapper himself, he can graduate more delicately their opposed effects. An experienced trainer will never stimulate more movement from behind than he can easily contain it in front. His aim at this stage is to get the horse to obey the alternate discreet touches of the tapper and restraining effects of the rein by increasingly compacting his frame as he continues to trot in very short steps, and to achieve a constant contact that is neither too light nor too strong.

The cautious procedure just described can rarely be skipped. Trying to obtain the piaffe initially from the walk or from the halt entails the risk of the horse learning to root his feet to the ground or

Figure 53: *Tapping the lower hindlimb area* **a** = *The hock;* **b** = *The fetlock*

even to move backwards, resistances which are extremely difficult to eradicate once the horse has discovered them. A good piaffe must always contain a tendency to forward movement be it by no more than a few centimeters. This is why the preparatory work at the trot is so important; admittedly it obliges the trainer to remain on the move all the time, but the effort is worthwhile.

Enormous progress will have been achieved when the length of the trotting steps can be reduced to the utmost (to half steps), without loss of impulsion. The periods of trotting can then be shortened but after the period at halt, the horse must immediately resume the shortened, springy trot, encouraged at first by the tapper. After a few strides, he is again halted. The purpose of the very frequent transitions from shortened trot to halt and vice versa is to make the horse attentive, sensitive and submissive. During the halt, one stands in front of the horse and rewards him for his immobility with a treat, while getting him to relax by praising him with gentle caresses and pats on the neck. These pauses may sometimes be necessary for the trainer also! At the end of the interval of halt, one quickly stands aside at the level of the horse's shoulder and encourages him to resume the active short trot. Clicking with the tongue and making just a sign with the tapper is usually sufficient encouragement.

Need it be said that the whole of this rather time-consuming process must be carried out with great calm. The shortened trot must remain lively and springy and may sometimes have to be animated by touches of the tapper, but the rein tension must remain light and constant.

The work may be tiring for the trainer, but is much more strenuous for the horse (ten minutes of knee bending gymnastics taxes the strength of the muscles of the thighs much more than an hour's walking exercise). The horse's endurance must be considered and the work must never be continued until fatigue sets in.

Once the horse has understood and accepted his trainer's requirement, it is time to observe the manner of the trot and to consider how it can be improved. One should have by then found out the most sensitive of the points on the hind limb that can be stimulated by the touches of the tapper. One must note whether the hind feet engage sufficiently or, on the contrary, too much, and in view of this determine which further action to take.

Touches of the tapper on the posterior surface of the thigh, between the stifle and the point of the hip have an animating and impulsive effect on the whole mechanism of movement. Stimulation of the lower regions, hock or fetlock joints, brings about more advancing

142

of the feet under the mass . However, other points of contact, the croup for example, may sometimes elicit more desirable reactions. On the other hand, a tendency to advance the hind feet exaggeratedly can be prevented by touching the anterior surface of the limb. One must be guided by practice and experience.

The most important thing, however, is weight distribution. Excessive tightening of the side reins causes too much weight to be thrown onto the shoulders and makes it almost impossible for the horse to pick up his fore feet; the insufficiently loaded hindquarter will then respond to the taps by stepping too high and too quickly.

If, on the contrary, the excessive lightening of the forehand leads to over-engagement and overloading of the hindquarters, one must stop using the tapper.

The appropriate equilibrium has to be established by taking into careful consideration the conformation of the horse and by lowering or elevating his head and neck with the leading rein. "Repetitio est mater studiorum" (repetition is the mother of learning). This maxim applies especially to work in hand—with respect to the trainer as much as to the horse. The effect of repetition with association in the horse's mind of cause and consequences has to be patiently awaited. A generous reward is a potent incentive to work; offering a favorite tidbit to a horse cheers him up and can sometimes achieve results that cannot be obtained as easily or as quickly, if at all, by the aids of hands and legs, whip or spur. Those who know something about the training of circus horses can confirm this is a fact. It certainly does not mean that everything can be achieved by this method; nonetheless, it should not be rejected out of hand.

When the instantaneous transition from the halt to the trot in half-steps with undiminished impulsion and submission to the aids is volunteered by the horse and one feels that the steps can easily be shortened just a little more, intelligent combination of the taps with the restraining aid of the hand will then produce the first step of piaffe from the halt. Even then one should not demand that the piaffe be executed absolutely on the spot.

The degree of elevation of the forearm matters less than the lightness of the contact. The trainer on the ground with his left hand holding the lead rein should be able to feel the suppleness of the poll as well as if he were seated in the saddle. His hand must allow and even encourage a forward progression of about one hoof length at every step. A click of the tongue, a swishing of the tapper may suffice with a sensitive horse. However, if the feet are not picked up at all, it is often because the trainer weights too heavily on the lead rein, either unconsciously while he directs his attention exclusively to the activity of the hind feet or because he worries that the horse might try to get away. But at this stage of training, when the horse is easily collectible, capable of flexing without difficulty his poll and hind joints, the risk of him forcing the trainer's hand when asked to produce some very cadenced steps of piaffer is most unlikely so it is with a very light contact that he can be led.

Three to four lively diagonal steps are quite enough to start with. Gradual progression increases the horse's confidence and leads to much better results than inconsiderate pressing on to achieve a more spectacular movement. This succeeds only in overtaking the horse's mental and physical powers, in agitating him and jeopardizing the results already achieved at great cost to time and work.

A common mistake of those new to this work is to try to incite every single step with a touch of the tapper. This can so destroy the horse's sensitivity to the stimulating effect of this indispensable instrument that stronger and stronger taps are needed to produce a result until finally the horse becomes completely indifferent to the aid and cannot be persuaded to make even one step.

Continuous tapping can also give the horse the impression that he is being punished for all his goodwill and hard work (as the British rightly say: "Never spur a willing horse"). Applied to work in hand, the motto is: never tap a horse while he is stepping with every sign of application and goodwill. To guarantee the correct execution of the piaffe when mounted, in the work in hand once the horse has understood the requirement, he should be left as much as possible to continue stepping of his own free will without being annoyed by touches of the tapper. The tapper should be used only if the horse becomes lackadaisical or completely ceases to work; touching him with the tapper while the piaffe is in flow highly disturbs him.

In short: use the tapper with discretion to start the piaffe from the halt, and when it is established let the horse mark time without disturbing. Observe the steps and interfere only when necessary.

Knowledge and feeling are absolute requisites for work in hand; the sensitivity and temperament of the horse must be taken into account in respect of both aids and duration of the work. One horse may go into piaffe as soon as he feels the restraining effect of the left hand of the trainer. Another may need to be potently stimulated to stir him out of immobility, and have to be drawn forward by the left hand while activated from behind with the right hand.

In all lessons, including the piaffe, there are three stages:

a) the learning period;

b) the practicing period; and

c) the development of perfect proficiency.

So having first taught the horse to execute just a few steps of piaffe, we then give him time to develop the regularity of the movement, and finally we think of a means of achieving the greatest possible proficiency in the performance of this beautiful air of the high school.

The essential conditions of correctness are the activity to the hind limbs and a pronounced flexion of all the joints, but especially of hip and stifle. Consequently, the horse must appear noticeably higher at the withers than at the croup; his back must slant downwards and backwards. If the horse does not first set himself sufficiently on the haunches (there are horses used to being worked in hand that start to piaffe as soon as they see the trainer approaching without first retracting their mass backwards to bring the hind feet close enough to the center of gravity) he will step too much on the spot with the hind feet insufficiently engaged.

The result is that the hind feet tread actively and regularly, but behind the plumb line of the hip joint so that the hindquarters are not loaded enough to relieve the forehand of weight and enable the forefeet to be picked up at all. The croup is high and the horse is on the forehand. The means of correction have already been explained: touching the hind limb with the tapper and elevating the neck with the lead rein. Under saddle, the correct disposition of the weight of the rider is an important aid. In work in hand it may be helpful to touch the forearm with the sole object of depriving the horse for a moment of some support in front. It is an aid that should not be totally excluded, but much experience and adroitness is needed to touch at the right place and at the right moment. Inexpert use of this aid can result in a lengthening of the outline as the stimulated forelimb comes into support while the other one is lifted.

In exceptional cases, in order to further refine the piaffe, the trainer can use a whip as well as a tapper and get an assistant to lead the horse. The procedure is fraught with danger, though. Exceptional quickness of perception and sense of rhythm are needed to obtain the lifting of the diagonal foreleg and touch it on the appropriate spot and at the right moment. It often happens that, suddenly deprived of the habitual support of the foreleg, the horse protests by lashing out with it; it can also collapse over the fetlock. The method can agitate the animal so much and produce such disastrous results that it should never be tried except by the most skillful of specialists.

Instead of leaving their hind feet too far behind, some horses tend on the contrary to put them too far forward. It is sometimes because of a fault of conformation, such as sickle hocks for example, although when we contemplate training horses for the sophisticated movements of dressage we normally exclude those that would present us with difficulties due to conformation. Excessive advancing of the hind feet is not useful engagement and must be countered as soon as possible. With so much weight on the hindquarters, it is impossible for the hind feet to spring if they remain rooted to the ground.

When this happens, rather more forward movement must be allowed at each step and the tapper must be applied on the anterior surface of the hind limb.

Another difficulty we may have to cope with is lateral inward or outward deviation of the croup. The first thing to verify is the length of the side reins and the tension on the leading rein. Tapping a horse behind and inexorably holding him in front is like trying to hammer a nail into a stone wall. But it may be that the horse has not yet completely overcome his inherent crookedness which shows up again with the increased demands. If the croup tends to turn inwards, the best plan is to change the hand to which one usually works, and put the horse in a slight shoulder-in position, using the wall to prevent a turning out of the croup.

The reason for standing to the left side of the horse during work in hand is that this is the usual leading position. Furthermore, most of us find that we can handle the tapper with more adroitness with the right hand than the left. But when satisfactory results have been obtained in work to the left, one should change sides.

Another complication is a horse's refusal to move at all, or even to move backwards to try and escape the restraint. This usually happens when a horse has not been trained to trot in hand in shortened steps before trying to teach it to piaffe.

It is, of course, more convenient to stand on one spot and it may be difficult to run backwards while facing the horse in order to keep up with the speed of the trot; the lazy do not like to exert themselves and the less athletic do not like to expose themselves to possible ridicule. But one looks even more ridiculous when having to run forwards to reach with the tapper the hind legs of the horse that is running backwards. And when this happens, one has to pay dearly for one's sins for only means of correction is the work at the trot in hand described above.

Two more faults that are very difficult to correct are the swaying of the croup from side to side, and, the crossing of the forefeet.

In the case of the first, one can try placing the horse in a shoulder-in position with his outside hind against the wall and tapping the inside hind sideways in the direction of the outside one. One could also use pillars and an assistant to lead the horse, but maneges equipped with pillars no longer exist.

The second fault, the crossing of the forelegs, is considered by the FEI (Rule 117) to be more serious still. It can unlikely be corrected when it is due to a faulty conformation of the forelegs (base narrow). In mild cases, it may be possible to eradicate the fault by elevating the neck and drawing the horse forwards.

The old masters have always pointed out that execution of the piaffe absolutely on the spot is a common source of defects and that a forward progression even if by no more than a few centimeters should invariably be the rule: "Not to go forwards means to fall back."

If a horse is not capable of changing immediately from piaffe to collected trot, there must be something wrong with his piaffe. This is the reason why the transition from piaffe to trot is required twice in the Intermediate II.

The Mounted Piaffe

When the horse is pretty well versed in the piaffe in hand and can produce 10 to 12 steps of piaffe without much difficulty, a competent rider can then get astride but the first lessons are still conducted with the help of the trainer with tapper and lead rein. The rider at first should be as passive as possible; he must beware of overloading the hindquarters by leaning backwards and must establish a very light contact. Very gradually the direct aids of hands and legs are substituted for the indirect aids of tapper and lead rein. For a while the trainer remains in fairly close proximity, ready to intervene only if the horse fails to respond to the aids of the rider or if his energy flags.

The rider must learn to harmonize the effects of weight, legs and hand, and should have to resort as little as possible to whip and spurs. One must constantly bear in mind that it is the horse that must be seen to work and not the rider. "Everything moves except the horse's feet" is a humiliating consequence of too much effort on the part of the rider.

The habit of trying to exact every step with an accentuated leg effect or with the spur so quickly blunts the sensitivity of the horse that in a very short time the rider can exhaust himself with effort without succeeding in getting the horse to budge by even one step. The horse must know his business and understand the aids; actually, the main difficulty of obtaining the piaffe from the saddle is one of agreement of minds.

In principle and ideally the aids are the same as for the trot. First the transition to trot has to be obtained by appropriate pressure of both legs, then the trot must be sustained by the suppleness of the seat of the rider and the light contacts of his legs in rhythm with the movements of the horse's rib cage. If every step of the trot had to be wrested by strength of legs, a horse would soon stop moving.

For obvious reasons, it is easier for the horse and the rider to begin by practicing the movement close to the wall; it is easiest to ensure that he stays straight. The rider should not try to lower the croup by holding his hands up high. Besides overloading the hindquarters, he would thus also deprive the horse of the essential activity of his back muscles. Active elevation of his neck causes the horse to hollow his back and this makes engagement of the hind feet impossible. In the piaffe, the horse's back should be lightly convex or at least straight.

Provided he is not disturbed by his rider, a horse that has been prepared by properly understood work in hand will nearly always find out by himself the equilibrium appropriate to the piaffe and this should not then be modified by the rider.

In view of the greater responsiveness to the aids that a horse trained to this stage should have developed, if the rider has to intervene to produce more animation or greater regularity, he must do so with great tact. It is all too easy to disrupt the rhythm by untimely or clumsy actions and difficulty for the horse to restore it immediately.

Depending on the aptitude of the horse, the transition to piaffe can be from the collected trot, from the walk or from the halt. When equilibrium, regularity and activity are well established, it should be done away from the wall to prove that the horse is obeying the aids instead of just reacting out of habit to the proximity of the wall.

In order to produce better flexion of the hocks, in some cases it can be helpful to obtain the piaffe from a very collected rein back or even, after a transition to walk, from the collected canter.

A movement that may look like mere play but in reality is nothing of the sort is the pirouette at piaffe. It should not be attempted before the horse can easily do a good number of steps of a perfectly regular piaffe on the straight; then the turn will considerably improve the horse's balance and collection. But things can go wrong, as with the canter or walk pirouette, if the rider is more concerned about the shortness of the turn than the flow of the movement and throws the horse off balance by using exaggerated weight aids. Then, to protect himself, the horse has to abandon the piaffe.

The turn must be preceded by a few steps of piaffe on the straight in relative collection; excessive collection makes the beginning of the pirouette difficult and leaves no room for the increased collection required in the second half of the turn.

In the preparatory steps on the straight, the horse should be slightly bent and positioned inwards by firmer use of the outside leg aid and a bare minimum of rein effect. As the horse continues to piaffe, the first turning step will hardly be noticeable and, after the second one a quarter of a pirouette will have been achieved, quite enough for the first attempts. The horse should then be allowed to continue in piaffe on a straight line as if nothing at all strange had happened and he had turned as if by accident without noticing he was doing so. In the second stage of learning, two or three steps, each step being a turning one, can be requested. Thus, progressively one comes to the third stage, the complete pirouette at a perfectly regular piaffe. Although this movement has not yet been prescribed in dressage tests, it can greatly enhance the attractiveness of a free-style performance and is any case a valuable exercise for the development of the strength of the muscles of the hindquarters and the suppleness of the hind joints.

The Passage

The passage is one of the most aesthetically pleasing movements of the high school but it does require some special aptitude from a horse. The rider cannot compensate by his aids for a lack of keenness and zest for living on the part of the animal. The latter particularly needs a strong back and a natural capacity for elevation of the forehand. It is very difficult, if at all possible, to produce passage-like steps from a weak and languid horse; his impulsion wanes as soon as he cannot use the ground solely for the purpose of efficient forward progression.

Work in hand, or the assistance to the rider of a person on the ground, may help to elicit the first steps of passage; nonetheless, the aids for the passage have to come principally, and finally exclusively, from the rider. If the horse does not understand the aids, or does not heed them, all impulsion and elevation fade as soon as the indirect aids of tapper or whip disappear.

There are various methods of teaching the passage; an experienced rider soon discovers which of them is best suited to the horse that he is training. The classical method, but by no means the easiest one, consists in developing the passage from the piaffe by allowing the horse to move forward somewhat and change the supporting role of his hind limbs into a combined supporting and propulsive one under the influence of impulsion and a skillful combination of impulsive and restraining aids. This results at first in passage-like strides which gradually with repetition and more accentuated aids turn into passage proper. From the passage, the steps are increasingly shortened by the combined effect of hands and legs, until the horse can execute easily the transition from passage to piaffe. In this manner, the passage and the transition from passage to piaffe and vice versa, are developed at the same time.

This would appear to be the most logical method but it is not always successful because many horses training for advanced dressage these days do not possess good aptitudes for either passage or piaffe. In most cases, it is necessary to teach the piaffe and the passage separately—either the one or the other first—and to work on the difficult transition at a later stage, when the horse has mastered both movements.

It is possible to obtain the passage from the collected walk if the horse has a lot of impulsion and energy, but it is usually easier to develop it from the collected trot with which the passage has more affinity. The best way of obtaining the increased collection, elevation and cadence demanded is to work on serpentines, figures of eight, half pass and counter changes. If impulsion dwindles a little, it must be restored by frequent changes of speed over gradually shorter distances (but if it fades away altogether, one should spare oneself futile effort). The driving aids of the legs and the restraining but tactful aids of hand and seat have to be used almost simultaneously.

Whichever method one chooses, one should not ask for more than a very few good passage steps in the early stage of teaching the new movement; one must give the horse enough time to develop strength, equilibrium, rhythm, etc. If the rider is too greedy, the horse will be unable to sustain the marked cadence that characterizes the movement.

At a later stage, circles and large voltes on the short sides of the arena can be very helpful in developing the passage. They allow one to use the inside leg to greater effect; the preponderance of action of the inside leg is extremely important in the passage on curved lines or in half pass. If the outside leg makes itself felt more than the inside one, the passage immediately loses all cadence and elevation.

However, irregular steps are more likely on curved lines than on straight ones because of the unequal loading of the hind limbs. A symmetrical figure eight at a perfectly regular passage to both hands with a fluent change of bend is a convincing proof of conscientious work on the part of the rider.

In the passage, as in all movements, some horses will tend to drag their feet and others to hurry. With the more sluggish type one should think more of the trot than of the passage. In the attempt to obtain sufficient elevation, it is too easy to gradually extinguish the

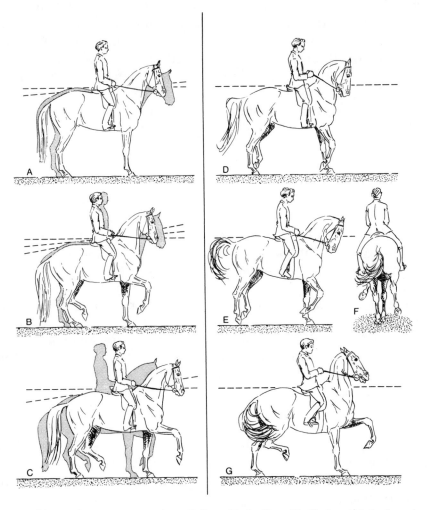

Figure 54: *Piaffe and passage.* **A** = *Collected halt;* **B** = *Piaffe showing the lowering of the croup;* **C** = *Imperfect transition to passage;* **D** = *Restrained by severe hands, the horse cannot pick up his forefeet;* **E** = *On the forehand;* **F** = *Hind feet turned out to escape loading; fidgety forefeet;* **G** = *Bad passage, showing tenseness, the horse above the bit, head and neck actively elevated, back hollow, feet snatched up.*

movement altogether. As soon as one feels a certain languor setting in, one should drive the horse forward with determination at the trot and try the passage again with rather more influence of legs and seat than of hand when impulsion and energy have been restored.

On the other hand, a tendency to hurry must be countered by half halts, at every stride if necessary. One should not think so much of slowing the speed as of preventing a transference of weight to the forehand which, of course, precludes elevation and cadence.

I will not discuss techniques involving the use of indirect aids, such as long reining, for example. They require good team work and more expertise and time than the dressage competitor possesses, and if the assistant is not an expert, more harm than good is the usual result.

But on the other hand, informed use of cavaletti can be of considerable assistance in obtaining and improving the passage. Informed, because even then one must be able to judge wisely the suitable distance between the cavaletti and especially the suitable height, taking into account the length of the collected steps of the particular horse and his capacity for elevation. The height at which the cavaletti are set should be increased extremely gradually. But for a feeling and effective rider they can be used to great advantage for developing cadence and equilibrium in the collected trot and the passage.

However, like all indirect aids, they must be used only occasionally and then for no more than a few minutes at a time. They will have proved their usefulness when they can be dispensed with.

A word again about the concept of suppleness. Why teach a horse suppleness when so much muscular tension is going to be needed eventually for collection? How can one expect a horse to be relaxed at the passage? The answer is that ease of movement or suppleness never implies a complete loss of tension but rather a complex, smooth alteration of shortening and lengthening of fibers of opposing muscles. In order to show ease, the horse has to use very actively indeed the strongly elastic muscles of his back and hindquarters. On one side then on the other the muscles must allow themselves to be unresistingly stretched by the action of their opposing muscles. A tense horse tautens the muscles of both sides simultaneously and although he may be able to project himself high off the ground, his passage is jerky and devoid of grace.

In this sense, suppleness implies a high degree of strength and elasticity of muscles, essential in all highly collected movements, but especially the passage. It is, therefore, correct to say that a high degree of collection requires a high measure of suppleness.

The ultimate result should be such perfect submission to light aids that the horse not only produces the passage or the piaffe whenever the rider desires, but also that he responds instantly to fine differences in the use of the aids by moving out of a piaffe almost on the spot to a well collected, flowing passage, and then back to piaffe. When this acute sensitivity and total responsiveness to the aids is achieved, the transitions from one air to the other should be perfectly fluent.

But for all the ability of the rider, this ideal is not always obtainable from the horses generally preferred in the modern sport of dressage, especially at the lower levels of competition, that is, naturally, long striding horses capable of spectacular extension. They seldom have good aptitudes for passage or piaffe.

Conversely, horses with very favorable aptitudes for passage and piaffe are not necessarily a safe bet for success at the higher levels of competition, because they lack the ability to extend their gaits in a sufficiently impressive manner. This is nothing new. There have always been horses from which one or another of the advanced movements of dressage can never be obtained despite all the knowledge, experience, talent and perseverance of their rider. Those of us with long experience of training horses for dressage recognize the limits set by nature and do not feel that failure to produce a winner every time reflects their competence.

Omnia praeclara rara sunt = Absolute perfection in all things is rarely possible!

Chapter 14

Lunging

This chapter on the subject of lunging does not purport to be a comprehensive discussion of all aspects of the work; it covers some details which are of more interest to the advanced rider than to the novice.

Lunging may seem to be a simple enough procedure, but the appearance of simplicity is deceptive. It is not sufficient to know how to lunge; one must also understand the purpose of the exercise. There are few riders these days who do and who are properly taught the technique, and many who do not appreciate how much there is to learn.

There are more and more insufficiently competent and knowledgeable riders who want to buy a horse as soon as possible and train him themselves. In the past they would spend some years learning to ride on schooled horses before venturing to undertake the education of their own from scratch.

People sometimes seem to believe that if the animal is their property, they are entitled to do as they please with him and do not see why they should pay for the advice of some busybody who thinks he knows best. There are proprietors of riding schools who countenance this attitude and turn a blind eye to ill-treatment which they will say is really in the province of societies for the prevention of cruelty to animals.

Even in riding schools a new owner may see that lunging for exercise is often delegated to ignorant stable lads or lasses who just chase the animal on a circle with loud cracks of the whip, without often bothering with cavesson, side reins, saddle or surcingle, bandages, etc. Emboldened by their example, he may conclude that the task requires little intelligence or experience and that he can just as well perform it himself. He may not even have been shown how to hold the whip or the lunge line, and when he decides to change hand, if he dares to do so, he risks becoming entangled in the lunge, or he may let go of the whip and let it lie down on the ground to pick it up again only after the horse has trodden on it a number of times.

It may be difficult to believe that such things do happen, but I can assure readers that lunging is often done so badly as to make a knowledgeable trainer feel sick.

But as long as anybody may buy a horse to keep at home or to rent a stall for him, nothing can be done to alter this state of affairs. It is not generally appreciated that skillful handling of animals is not instinctive; it must be learned but there are few schools with enough personnel and equipment to provide the training.

A time may come when a license will be required to own, ride or train a horse, and when all horses will be treated not like automations, but creatures of flesh, blood, nerves and mind. Sometimes I think that would be a fine idea.

However, to return to the present subject, let us first consider the different purposes of lunging:

1. To prepare the unbroken horse for the task of carrying a rider.

2. To supple a horse before a lesson; to exercise a convalescent one; to produce a horse suitable for teaching novice riders.

3. For corrective purposes, (i.e. relaxing of certain parts of the body, improvement of lateral suppleness or of obedience).

Regarding the first reason, all trainers accept that lunging is an essential preparation for mounted work. However, before starting to lunge a horse, one should have made some assessment of conformation and temperament and in the light of those facts have come to a provisional judgment of the horse's prospects.

It is a great mistake to let the first lunging lessons be carried out by even an experienced groom until by force of habit the horse has become resigned to running round on a circle. One can fail to notice the peculiarities of movement of the animal concerned. The roots of future difficulties can often be traced back to faults and omissions in this early stage of training which can just as well spoil a horse as improve him.

Familiarizing a horse with the equipment, choosing the most suitable place, deciding on the desirability or not of an assistant, on the length of the lesson, the time to change hand, is altogether the task of an expert. From the very beginning one should be able to judge the action of the hind limbs and the activity of the back muscles of the horse, the setting of his neck, the coupling of head and neck, the activity of the mouth—all things that have to be taken into account when deciding on the length of side reins, the height at which to buckle them to the surcingle or saddle, and whether to use a snaffle or not in addition to a cavesson (Figure 56).

The handling of the whip is extremely important. One must avoid frightening the young horse. He has to be taught to accept this extension of the trainer's arm, to understand its significance, to respect

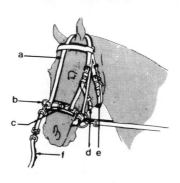

Figure 55: *Lunging cavesson.* **a** = *Nose strap;* **b** = *Central pivoting ring;* **c** = *Immovable ring for the attachment of side rein when a snaffle bit is not used;* **d** = *Cheek piece;* **e** = *Throat latch;* **f** = *lunge line.*

it, yet not to fear it. Inexpert or impatient whip lashers can do great harm and a whip shy horse is always a reflection of the incompetence of his first trainer.

For the very first lunging lessons, when a horse can be expected to react most undesirably, it is advisable to be assisted by two or three helpers. The horse ought never to be in a position that allows him to get away with misbehavior. Furthermore, it is essential for the trainer to be able to maintain constant eye contact with the equine pupil; it is a well established fact that a young horse will stop or turn around as soon as this eye contact is lost.

In most cases, but especially with horses that are rather stiff at the poll, it is better not to buckle the side reins to the snaffle in the hope of improving the suppleness of this region. Rather than flex at the poll, the horse is much more likely to evade in some way pressure on the sensitive tongue and bars. This is how the roots of ineradicable mouth difficulties are thus sown, such as lifting the tongue or protruding it to one side to shield the bars, opening the mouth, head nodding, etc.

The side reins should then be buckled to the fixed side rings of the cavesson and adjusted to a length short enough to produce some flexion of the poll, but not so short as to cause discomfort or impair proper forward movement. The flexibility of the poll can gradually be improved by progressive shortening of the side reins. As a result of the flexion, the inviolable mouth, untrammelled by steel, will be able to produce the relaxed movement called chewing of the bit that massages the parotid glands and gets them to retract into the neck.

The cavesson, of course, must fit perfectly and be firmly held in place as for work in hand. Elastic insets in the side reins are definitely not advisable with horses that resist the flexion at the poll; they must learn that they cannot escape the reasonable constraint of the side reins except by relaxing their tightly contracted neck muscles.

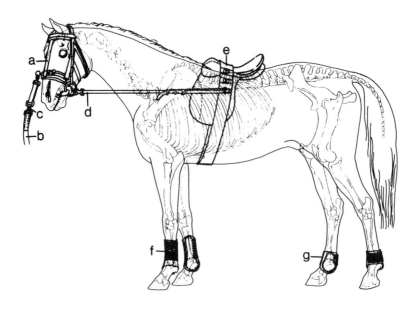

Figure 56: *Equipment for lunging:* **a** = *Cavesson;* **b** = *Lunge rein;* **c** = *Swivel;* **d** = *Side rein;* **e** = *Surcingle with rings at various heights for attachment of side reins;* **f, g** = *Brushing boots.*

Regarding the second purpose, every lunging lesson (except when used for teaching a novice rider or restoring the strength of a convalescent horse) must serve to improve carriage, action and suppleness. The horse will not improve of his own accord by being allowed to run any old way on a circle. On the contrary, there is hardly a horse that cannot be improved by systematic work on the lunge. The speed of the trot, the straightness of the horse at canter left or right can benefit, even a somewhat unsatisfactory walk can be ameliorated by getting the lunged horse to step over cavaletti placed at suitable distances on the circle. There are always possibilities of improvement, and lunging for this purpose may be an absolute necessity when for some reason or another one cannot give the animal his usual hour of lesson under saddle.

Regarding the third reason, over time a horse worked under saddle can develop covert ways of shirking honest movement so gradually that they are not perceived by riders who do not concentrate on overall movement or cannot feel it. These covert resistances can eventually culminate in overt resistance in the form of stopping, deviating from the prescribed track, suddenly turning round, or running backwards, or even rearing and lashing out with a foreleg .

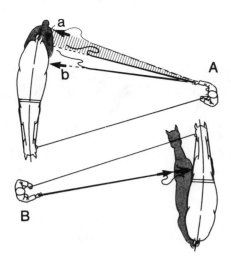

Figure 57: *Effect of the lunging whip.* **A** = *In the direction of the hindquarters to quicken the movement;* **a** = *From behind towards the point of the buttocks;* **b** = *Towards the hindquarters at about the point of the hip.* **B** = *In the direction of the shoulder to prevent an unwanted diminution of the circle.*

Lunging is the best remedy. When a horse is unhampered by the weight of the rider, it is much easier to get him to understand that his main duty always is to move forward diligently in regular steps.

But lunging work for the latter purpose can lead to success only if it is conducted by a trainer with sufficient experience in correcting spoiled horses; it demands total unflappability, great firmness, patience and consistency.

No good can come of it if the lunger finds the business so tedious that he needs to chat with a circle of admiring acquaintances while the horse is going round on the circle. From the first minute of the lesson to the last, the horse must remain attentive to the aids: the lunge line in steady contact, the whip always at the ready, the voice that scolds or praises, the constant eye contact. Sometimes it may help to have an assistant. Even then one may have to wait a long time to achieve satisfactory results. Much depends on the stage of education of the horse and on how long he has been allowed to get away with his sins.

Long reining can be much more effective than lunging, especially with horses that obstinately turn around. It also helps to improve lateral suppleness. However, it does require a fair amount of skillfulness and before attempting to long rein a tricky horse it is highly advisable to achieve sufficient expertise by practicing first with one that is already easy to maneuver with two reins, and then introduce the

Figure 58: *Lunging a young horse with side reins attached to the snaffle. Correct way of holding lunge and whip; suitable length and height of side reins.*

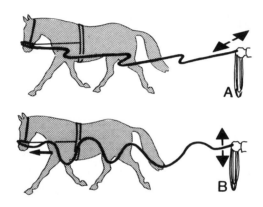

Figure 59: **A** = *Vibrating the lunge to quicken the speed;* **B** = *Sending waves along the lunge to enlarge the circle.*

Figure 60: *The right way to hold the lunge and whip when standing by the horse's head at the halt.*

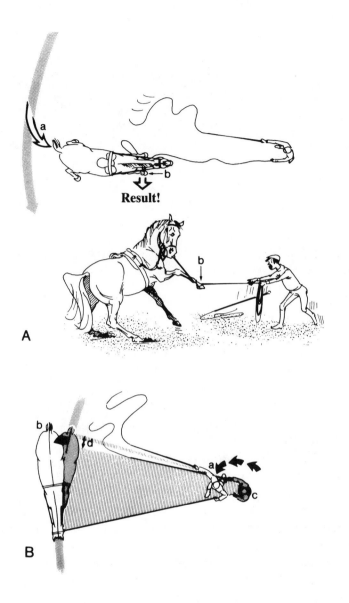

Figure 61: *Wrong lunging procedures.* **A** = *Threatening his horse with the whip with the result that* **a** = *He suddenly turns inwards; and,* **b** = *He gets a forefoot caught in the lunge.* **B** = *The trainer runs round on the circle with the horse;* **a, b** = *The horse deviates outwards from the circle with his hindquarters;* **c, d** = *Correct position of the horse on the circle.*

system to a horse that behaves well on the single lunge. Much more adroitness is needed to long rein than one might imagine.

The extra time and effort needed to master the technique is well

Figure 62: *Long reining.* ----- **a** = *Outside rein too high, rubbing the underside of the dock;* ----- **b** = *Outside rein too loose, rubbing the fetlock;* —— = *Correct length and position of outside rein.*

rewarded in the end by the facility with which the change of hand which can be done without interruption of forward movement to readjust the now unnecessary side-reins.

It is a great shame that the arts of lunging and long reining are neglected by so many riders nowadays. They would help themselves, as well as their horses, to make quicker progress if they accepted the necessity of a thorough education in those important elements of good horsemanship.

When the rider has achieved proficiency in the art of long reining, lateral movements, pirouettes, flying changes, even piaffe and

passage are possible in long reins with a horse that knows those movements. In the higher education of the horse, long reining is a very useful subsidiary aid to supple a horse that has lost impulsion as a result of excessively prolonged collected work under saddle.

But I have yet to meet a rider willing to admit that he ever overworks a horse... though, of course, there are *others* who do!

Chapter 15

The School Horse

A treatise on dressage would be incomplete if no mention were made of "School Horses" and "School Riding." The terms are seldom used or understood nowadays. In what way is a School Horse different from a normally schooled horse? What does High School mean?

For the sake of clarity, we should answer the last question first. A High School Horse is one that has been trained to achieve the highest possible degree of flexion of the haunches. It is this utmost flexibility that enables the horse to be absolutely at the command of the rider and to perform extraordinary feats of agility.

A High School Horse is totally submissive, perfectly easy to collect and instantly responsive to aids so light that they are invisible to the spectator.

Easier said than done. If one has never tried to train a horse to such an extreme degree of submission, one cannot imagine how interesting but highly demanding the work is and how long the training has to last, even when a horse has the exceptional aptitudes required. In any case, one would never contemplate beginning to train an horse to this end if he did not possess extraordinary aptitudes. It would be an utter waste of time and effort.

To be worth consideration as a High School prospect, a horse must already have more that normally supple haunches and intensive impulsion.

Haunches is a vaguely understood term. Some riders think that it is just another name for hindquarters; others think that it means hocks, and others apply it to the whole system of stifle, hock and fetlock.

But that is not how it was understood by masters of the classical period of horsemanship. For them the haunches comprised exclusively the biggest joints of the hind limbs, i.e. the hip and stifle joints. This explains why some horses with rather straight hocks are able to perform easily the most difficult dressage movements.

There are people who object to dressage because they say that the collected movements impair the soundness of hocks. We must let the veterinary profession decide whether this assertion is well founded, but spavins are frequently found in horses that have never been asked to move in collection. If it is true that dressage can injure the hocks, the more likely cause of trauma could be the abnormal straightening of the joint in extended trot and canter; exaggerated extension is often seen these days and is unfortunately much too highly rated by judges.

However, damaged hocks are not often found in dressage horses that have not been put to work at too early an age and have been progressively and sensitively schooled. The stallions of the Spanish Riding School of Vienna, despite the high degree of collection demanded of them, show no signs of spavin and some continue to work brilliantly up to the age of 25 or 30. On the other hand, it is a fairly common affliction of the show jumpers.

This is what Gustav Steinbrecht, one of the most esteemed dressage trainers of the XIXth century, wrote about collection in his *Gymnasium des Pferdes*:

"Most of the strength required to propel and support the body of a horse resides in its haunches and it is principally to the development and control of the strength of this region that the horsemaster must devote his attention. There are many trainers and riders who talk much about obtaining the flexion of the haunches and who imagine that they are working to that effect, but have never once experienced the feeling imparted by an actual flexion of haunches. They do not seem to realize that there are two joints above the hock which are much bigger and more important that the latter and if they achieve only mediocre results is because of their failure to obtain more flexion from the hock downwards. Hundreds of horses with powerful haunches are prematurely fatigued because the power of those perfectly designed parts has never been utilized as it should be in order to take weight off the forelegs and to safeguard the inferior joints of the hind legs."

"It is certainly not easy to flex powerful haunches, precisely because of their strength. The mightiest of riders can never overcome their resistance to flexion by the use of brute force. This can succeed in damaging severely the back and hocks of the horse, but it is of absolutely no avail against the incomparably greater power of a horse's haunches. Getting a horse to flex its haunches will always remain the privilege of an educated, experienced and tactful horseman who knows how by progressive and systematic work he can transform the vertebral column of the animal into a serviceable lever that will give him the mechanical advantage. The uninformed, inexpert rider who relies only on the strength will remain unable to obtain the compliance of the horse's haunches and will either ruin its hocks or have to depend entirely on its mood."

"Masters of the past were extraordinarily skillful in getting a horse to flex its haunches. Without visible effort, they obtained from their horses wonderful feats of agility; they transformed utilitarian equitation into an art of inspiring beauty; those of us who want this art to survive untarnished... must learn to follow their ways."

This was written in 1844! And the principles remain the same.

However, up to a point, the training of the School Horse is no different from the training of any horse for service under the saddle. It is all a matter of equilibrium. Thus, the primary education of the School Horse proceeds through various stages which are:

a) At the beginning of his education under saddle, the young horse (or any uneducated horse) supports the greater proportion of his own weight and that of his rider on the forehand: the back slants downward from back to front.

b) The good "all-rounder" or the dressage horse at novice and elementary level moves in horizontal equilibrium, with the weight supported equally by hind and forelegs; the back is horizontal.

c) In collection, the horse at medium and advanced level carries more weight on the hind legs than the forelegs, the haunches are moderately flexed, the back slants slightly downwards.

d) The highly proficient dressage horse, the School Horse, flexes his haunches pronouncedly and carries substantially more weight on the hindquarters than on the forehand; the back inclines noticeably downwards.

To "school" a horse therefore means to teach him gradually by means of special exercises to flex his haunches to the possible limit imposed by anatomy. This limit is obviously variable; nevertheless, it can be said that a moderate degree of collection can be demanded as soon as a horse has learned to move regularly and actively at the working trot, when he no longer offers resistance to the flexion of the poll, when the masculature of the top line of the neck is suitably developed, when he can be equally and evenly bent from head to tail on both sides. Work on serpentines, on small circles, on exact voltes of six meters and the various lateral movements accustom the horse to increased loading of one hind limb, the one on the side of the bend.

When the horse can perform those exercises with ease, a superior degree of collection without diminution of impulsion can be demanded, in which both hind legs are simultaneously loaded by being made to tread closer to the center of gravity as a result of the timely opposition of the hand to the forward movement stimulated by the rider's legs; it is the increased flexion of the haunches that produces the relative elevation of the forehand.

The result is achieved by:

increased coordination of the effects of outside rein and inside leg, thus limiting lateral bend and increasing collection and elevation of the forehand;

transitions that improve collection, half and complete halts, riding in position and counter-position, counter-canter, lateral movements, pirouettes at the walk, the rein back, the *Schaukel*;

the flying change and then flying changes at set intervals. They are not collecting exercises, but it is at this stage of schooling that they are introduced;

the canter pirouette, which demands the highest degree of collection that can be obtained at canter;

collected work in hand.

A horse of what used to be called the "Low School" would have honorably completed his education through all the above stages. As a result, his haunches would be so amenable that he could produce without difficulty the "School Halt," the "School Position," the "School Rein Back" and the "School Gaits" which still need to be concisely defined. Piaffe and passage would come later and were considered to be lessons of the High School (which previously also included the Airs Above the Ground).

However, dressage experts and authors are not in complete agreement as to which movements comprise the High School. Some consider that all the collected gaits and the pirouettes belong to the High School but not the flying changes (Watjen is of this opinion). But the XIXth century masters of the classical school would include as Airs of the High School on the Ground only the piaffe and the passage. Among modern authors, there are some who count piaffe, passage and all flying changes of canter, including the changes at every stride (a tempo), as Airs on the Ground of the High School, but not the pirouette and the collected gaits.

It would be pointless to enter into a further discussion of those fine points, but one may be allowed to point out that if the flexion of the haunches is the hallmark of the High School then the flying changes of canter should not be included because even the changes at every stride do not require a high measure of collection. In fact, they are more fluently executed when the horse is allowed to move in horizontal equilibrium. On the other hand, without a high degree of collection and flexion of haunches, correct pirouettes are inconceivable.

After having thus digressed, we can now analyze the characteristics of the School Movements.

The School Halt

A school halt is not possible before the haunches have been completely brought under the control of the rider (Figure 63). On both sides, the hoofs of the hind feet must align at the vertical of the respective hip joint. The hindquarters must support the greater proportion of the weight and the horse, while continuing to chew the bit, must remain perfectly still on a light contact, with the neck elevated and flexed at the poll.

Figure 63: *The School Halt.* **a** = *Lowered croup;* **b** = *Flexed haunches;* **c** = *Imaginary plumb line running from the hip joint to the toe of the hind hoof.*

The horse must maintain this very collected stance with unaltered flexion of hind joints until the rider yields the contact. If on the contrary, the rider increases the tension on the reins (as if he were about to rein back, for example), the horse must submissively flex his haunches even more. The resulting position is what used to be called the School Position.

The School Position

The School Position can be compared to a human stance with bent knees (Figure 64). The angles of the hind joints are closed and are like strong springs compressed by weight and ready to expand as soon as they are permitted to do so. A very slight advance of hands combined with driving aids is sufficient to produce forward movement instantaneously. The immediate transitions to collected trot or canter from the halt or the rein back are proof of the submission of the haunches.

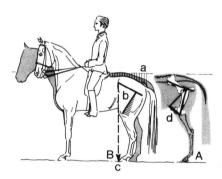

Figure 64: *The School Position.* **A** = *Normal stance of hind legs in the transition to halt.* **B** = *The School position;* **a** = *Lowered croup;* **b** = *Flexion of haunches;* **c** = Plumb line from hip joint.*

The Rein Back

In the advanced tests, the rein back must be executed in a high state of collection, with the croup lowered and neither hind leg deviating from a perfectly straight line. Each rearward step demands even more flexion of haunches which means that the steps have to become progressively shorter. The springs are thus compressed more and more allowing for instantaneous forward movement at the gait prescribed the moment the hand yields and the legs make themselves felt.

The classical rein back is a movement that we are seldom privileged to observe.

Figure 65: *Classical rein back out of which instantaneous forward movement is obtained.* **a** = *Lowered croup;* **b** = *Flexion of haunches.*

The School Gaits

The School Gaits are more cadenced than the normal collected gaits. The haunches are more flexed and consequently the steps are shorter, very springy and the feet are more pronouncedly lifted. Impulsion must project the body more upwards rather than forward. The School Gaits are much more arduous than the normal collected ones and it is understandable that a horse will at first attempt to subside gradually or even suddenly into a flatter, less strenuous manner of moving. Therefore, one should not therefore demand more than a few steps at a time, especially at the beginning; the horse must be allowed to develop the inordinate strength required by repetition and daily practice, but on no account should he be made to continue working in such an exhausting manner beyond the onset of fatigue.

If the steps become irregular, according to circumstances one can either allow a pause to allow the horse to recover energy, or restore the state of collection by executing a transition to halt or a rein back, and bring the work to an end after just a few more good forward steps.

The work should be done first and foremost at the School Trot; the School Walk is then developed from the School Trot, but must never be prolonged; it is best to use it only for a few steps between periods at the School Trot, or just to prepare another movement, like the passage, for example. The School Canter comes last.

The School Trot

The characteristics of the School Trot are regularity, energy and

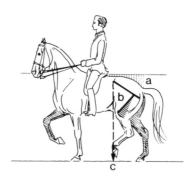

Figure 66: *The School Trot.* **a** = *Lowering of the croup;* **b** = *Flexion of haunches;* **c** = *Plumb line from hip joint.*

distinct cadence. Slow, tense, hovering steps do not amount to a School Trot and, since they are caused by insufficient activity of the back muscles, the neck should not be elevated beyond a point that brings the nose to a higher level than the hip joint. Active elevation of the neck always entails the risk of impairing the activity of the back muscles. It is always advisable to occasionally allow the joints of the hindquarters to extend powerfully by changing from the highly collected trot to medium trot and from medium trot to return to School Trot.

Overloading the hindquarters by too strong rein tension, or a rein effect unduly prolonged, incapacitates them and extinguishes impulsion. In horsemanship, cadence means equal proportion between moments of suspension and moments of support. Excessive elevation approximating an almost vertical position of neck and nose brings about a disproportion between the propulsive and carrying powers of the hindquarters. As a result, the steps of the forelimbs become jerky and the hind steps degenerate into a vague sort of walk.

The School Walk

The School Walk is a gait that is of no practical use except as a preparation for another collected movement. It is purely a means to an end and no more than a few strides should ever be demanded. One should never try to obtain it before a horse can be collected easily at the walk. It requires extraordinary precision in the use of the aids; a rather accentuated but short transition must be immediately succeeded by an impulsive action of the leg. Driving with the leg and seat and simultaneously checking with the hand confuses the horse so much that instead of flexing his haunches he will run away with the rider.

170

Of all the gaits, the most difficult one to produce is an absolutely pure School Walk, that is, with lively, expressive steps, in clearly marked perfectly regular four beats. A rider who is not exceptionally well schooled and experienced should not attempt it; experimentation can result in irreparable flawing of the walk.

Figure 67: *The School Walk.* **a** = *Lowering of the croup;* **b** = *Flexion of haunches;* **c** = *Plumb line from the hip joint.*

The School Canter

The School Canter is also quite tricky. The canter must always be lively and springy, and the School Canter particularly so. Too much collection and shortening of the strides suppresses the springiness of the gait. The ultimate result of a rider's incompetent efforts at slowing the canter is a listless movement of no value at all. The School Canter, though shorter than a normally collected canter, must be even more springy. Since the hindquarters are always more loaded in the canter than in the trot, a School Canter entails the maximum possible flexion of the haunches. A classical School Canter with undiminished impulsion is the hallmark of supreme horsemanship. It alone permits the gracefully springy, perfectly regular School Pirouette with extremely lowered croup, "on a soup plate" as the expression goes, a movement that is undisputedly impractical in a normally collected canter wherein some ground has to be gained at every stride to preserve the purity of the gait.

Nonetheless, the purity of the gait is also what matters most in the School Pirouette and it is, of course, much more difficult to maintain it than in pirouettes at levels of dressage below Grand Prix. As a result, in a Grand Prix test, a School Pirouette executed from start to finish at a perfectly regular canter has to be very highly rated.

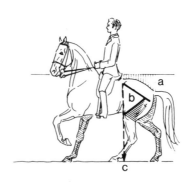

Figure 68: *The School Canter.* **a** = *Lowered croup;* **b** = *Flexion of haunches;* **c** = *Plumb line from hip joint*

Piaffe and Passage

Piaffe and passage complete the education of the School Horse. They have already been discussed at length in the previous chapter, but here we will consider the coordination of aids. There are three possibilities: legs first, then hands; or the reverse; or hands and legs simultaneously. The choice must depend on the state of equilibrium of the horse in the preceding movement just before the transition.

If the horse is in horizontal equilibrium, hands and legs act practically simultaneously. If too much weight is on the forehand, the legs must act first to engage the hindquarters before these can be loaded by the transition. In this case, it is legs first, then hands.

If the horse is already well collected, forehand elevated and hindquarters well engaged, it is unnecessary to produce more engagement. Tactful opposition of the hands to forward movement will bring the submissive horse to the halt; the rider just keeps his legs in soft contact with the horse's sides, ready to prevent lateral deviation of the croup.

The same principles apply when the higher degree of collection required has to be preserved in forward movement.

The elevation of the forehand is not obtained simply by actively lifting up the head and neck with the reins. It has to be the result of increased engagement of the hindquarters produced by the driving aids, combined with control of speed by the opposition of the hands. The limit of this opposition is determined by the amount of flexion at the poll the horse can comfortably bear.

The ultimate result of all the careful schooling is pronounced engagement of the hindquarters, elevation of the neck and absolute steadiness of the flexion at the poll.

The neck by now is so firmly connected to the back that loading or unloading of the hindquarters and the proportionate equilibrium of their carrying and propelling functions can be determined by its position.

When is a horse ready for the High School? Well, perfect

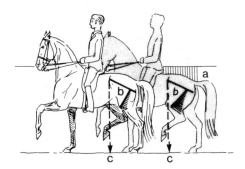

Figure 69: *Classical Piaffe.* **a** = *Lowered croup;* **b** = *Flexion of haunches;* **c** = *Plumb line from hip joint.*

submission in the transitions to halt from all three gaits (even extended trot) is the most reliable indication that the time has come to begin High School education. If the horse stays calmly on the bit at the standstill without disengaging his hindquarters by shifting them sideways or by lifting up the croup, he can be deemed to be ready for the high degree of collection that characterizes the High School.

When horsemanship was generally considered to be an art worthy of the most serious study, the High School was intended to demonstrate how much a skillful rider could demand from a horse methodically schooled according to certain firmly established principles.

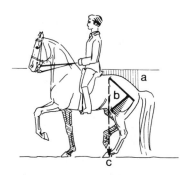

Figure 70: *Classical Passage.* **a** = *Lowered croup;* **b** = *Flexion of haunches;* **c** = *Plumb line from hip joint.*

But the same principles had to be applicable to the education of the saddle horses in general without rendering them unsuitable for military service; a horse was never specialized for the High School before he had become a good "campaign" horse. According to Seeger for example, writing in the middle of the nineteenth century, the campaign horse had to be so perfectly "schooled" that he would submit graciously to all reasonable requirements on the part of the rider, be strong and supple enough to execute easily the collected movements and yet be satisfactory for the chase and the fastest cavalry charge.

In answer to those who maintain that a horse trained for dressage is useful for all other purposes, one can quote an example from more recent times (cited by Ch. v. Losh, author of *Die Jagd in Rot*, a book about hunting). "In 1906, one of the participants in the Kaiser prize, an annual long distance ride of 152 km, was the celebrated dressage rider Lieutenant Waltzer on a Hanoverian horse that had been worked exclusively in the manege for six years up to the day of the competition. They were among the first to pass the winning post although the horse had not been given any special training for the event. It did not need it because it had been so well muscled up by High School work."

A "schooled" horse ought never to be purely a work of art and a show beast. It must always remain a horse that can be ridden across country with unalloyed pleasure. This is why (in Germany) at the lower levels of dressage, at the end of the test in the dressage arena a horse has to jump an obstacle from both sides, and his manner of jumping has a considerable influence on his placing. This is also why in the higher classes up to and inclusive of the Grand Prix Special, impulsion and maximum range of stride in the basic gaits (extended walk, trot and canter) earn such high marks. A coefficient of 2 is applied to the extended walk and, for reasons already mentioned, to the pirouette (but not any longer to piaffe and passage).

But these days, it is only on the race course that a schooled horse's speed can be properly tested. We do not have the extensive exercise grounds that were always provided in addition to the riding halls for the training of the military campaign horse. Nevertheless, the concept of versatility is preserved in modern dressage tests by the importance—albeit exaggerated—attached to the extended movements.

The lessons of the High School that demand extreme flexion of haunches, like the Airs Above the Ground, are practiced in only a few countries these days where horses of an antique type, like the Andalusians and the Lipizzaner, are still being bred. Those airs are not part of modern dressage because only horses of that particular type are capable of executing them. Because of the high marks obtainable in the extended movements, breeders are now trying to satisfy the demands of ambitious dressage riders by producing horses with a natural scope of movement unimaginable in the past.

It is therefore practically impossible to make a comparison between the ancient and the modern art of dressage. The requirements, the criteria, the system of judging are too different. Nevertheless, the aims and principles of present day schooling are pretty much the same as those that guided our ancestors.

Xenophon, a pupil of Socrates and the founder of the science of horsemanship, formulated the same aims and principles in 450 B.C. that are embodied these days in the regulations of the FEI. His following description of what is certainly the passage shows a remarkable feel for quality of movement: "If you teach your horse to hold his poll high and to flex his head and neck elegantly on the lightest possible contact, he will show all the conceit of a stallion in the presence of mares. With polls held high, head curbed, tail elegantly arched, he moves his legs in elevated, regular steps. When your horse moves in this manner, he is displayed in all his beauty and shows by his proud, eager, lofty bearing that nothing gives him more pleasure than to be ridden."

We should feel proud of having succeeded in preserving the main elements of the classical art of horsemanship and of having quickly discarded certain grotesque aberrations (like the canter on three legs, or the canter rearwards, etc.) of undoubtedly skillful horseman who cared, however, too little for the nature of the horse.

These days, the rider who can educate a horse to execute with ease all the movements prescribed in an Olympic Grand Prix is a worthy champion and interpreter of the traditional art of the High School.

Thanks to the efforts of the FEI and to the increasing international participation in advanced dressage events, unanimity of views and standards is becoming established among trainers, riders and judges.

The complete consensus of experts in any branch of science or art does not exist, and it cannot be expected in such a difficult one as ours. Nevertheless, general agreement regarding respect or infringement of principles is an urgent necessity because of the influence the opinions of judges of dressage tests exert on methods of training and breeding policies.

The science of breeding has made such progress that horses are now being produced of a quality that was inconceivable in the past. In the major studs of Germany and some other nations breeding stock is being selected with the aim of passing on to the progeny harmonious conformation, adaptability to all disciplines, natural impulsion, docility and endurance. But breeding will never be an exact science and it is too much to demand that every horse produced be perfect in nearly all respects.

Those top quality horses are understandably on the whole easier to school than their often unbelievably heavy ancestors. If only for aesthetic reasons, we should do them justice by applying ourselves very seriously to the task of schooling them patiently.

What the dressage rider should want to produce is a living work of art. The art of horsemanship may not be appreciated in our time as much as it used to be, but this is the fault of the beholder and not of the art. Contemporary society generally is too concerned with material possession and technology to find time to establish a close relationship with animals; it values more highly the artifacts of men than the transitory creations of nature. If it were a question of rescuing either a Rembrandt or a cat from a burning house, who would opt for the cat?

Still, if interest in artistic horsemanship can be sustained beyond the year 2000, one more aspect of our cultural heritage will have been saved from so much of the havoc of the twentieth century.